Adele Craven - Killer Mortician

Pete Dove

Published by Trellis Publishing, 2021.

While every precaution has been taken in the preparation of this book, the publisher assumes no responsibility for errors or omissions, or for damages resulting from the use of the information contained herein.

ADELE CRAVEN - THE KILLER MORTICIAN

PETE DOVE

The charges pursued against Adele Craven turned into to, at the time, one of the longest running and most expensive criminal cases in Cincinnati history. It is still a crime surrounded by uncertainty, despite confessions from three people. Adele's involvement is held, in many quarters, still in doubt.

Imagine she was not involved – the horror, the insanity of going through firstly the death of a spouse, followed by years of stress and tension. Ultimately facing the prospect of life in prison, or worse, the possibility of parole deep on the horizon while the most important people in your life, your children, grow up apart from you.

But if she was responsible for murder, and that is what the courts decided in the end, then how callous to take a father away from those children, to risk their upbringing, their security because of passion and dollars. For, in this case, the love of money really would be the route of all evil.

Adele Vicuna was born in 1963. For the young girl, the future appeared to offer little. Born to Hispanic parents in a working-class area of Long Beach, California, her early years were nothing special. A quiet, respectful girl; that she should now be a convict, guilty of murder, seems impossible to those who knew her back then.

But her story took on a series of twists. And the first of these was when she met Stephen Craven, a successful pilot from a middle-class background. For Adele, a dream future seemed assured. At the time, Stephen was working as a coast guard in Florida. But the two soon decided on marriage. When that happened, in 1989, it seemed as though life was perfect. Her first son, Daniel, soon appeared, and another, exciting change to her life followed quickly after.

Stephen got a job with Delta Airlines, and when they opened a hub inland, he signed up. In 1992 the couple moved to a rambling house in the well-off district of Carimel Ridge, in Edgewood Kentucky. The perfect family seemed to thrive.

Local reporter Jim Hannon describes the picture-perfect world of the new 'village' of Carimel Ridge, as sweet and succulent as the name sounds. 'The kind of place where you have backyard barbeques, and kids ride their bikes up and down the streets.'

They soon became established members of the local church. Something that would later be reported at Adele's trial. A juror on that trial, Stephanie Morton, spoke on the TV programme 'Snapped' which examines complex murder stories. She told of the impact their Adele and Stephen's church attendance made on her.

'They loved the lord, they loved the church. And they worked for that church.'

But by the time, three years later, that their second son was born, cracks were beginning to appear in the marriage. As a pilot, Stephen spent a lot of time away from home, working as he travelled around the globe. That left Adele with the challenging job of running the house and bringing up two young sons. She adored the boys, a neighbour Aimee Boyce stressing that she was 'an awesome mum' but she also adored the lifestyle having a pilot for a husband brought. When Stephen was home, he spent quality time with his sons and Adele was happy. But times away meant boredom, and that was addressed by spending money, buying expensive items for the house. By the time a decade had passed from their late 1980s marriage, they were in trouble.

They were not the first, and certainly not the last, couple for whom having one partner away and financial pressures made the normal differences of any marriage turn firstly into fissures, and then into deep cracks. Stephen not only became critical of his wife's spending, but also of her weight. Adele, naturally, was small of stature, and well built, He was happy to start arguments even in front of their friends. Aimee Boyce tells of a time when she was a guest in the home, and Stephen suddenly started on to Adele about her spending, about her eating. Criticism hurt, and the marriage began to fall apart.

Stephen was a controlling figure. He tried to keep a tight hand on the family finances and even disallowed Adele access to their account's credit card. But while faults existed on both sides, what was never in doubt was the couple's love for their children. Realising what was happening to their marriage, they sought guidance. Counselling helped, and for a while matters were much better.

Indeed, so much better that the couple decided to give the family a treat; it was now that Adele's life would take another twist, and this time one that led to a downward spiral which would end with her facing the death penalty for the murder of her husband. It was the dawn of the new Millennium, one that would fail to deliver its promises to Stephen and Adele, as well as their children. Daniel and his younger brother, Robert, were soon to lose their parents.

Russell 'Rusty' McIntire was just a few years younger than Adele. He was a baggage handler who worked for Delta, but who also possessed good handyman skills. Rusty McIntire also had psychological disorders. He could be compulsive, addictive and obsessive.

Stephen Craven heard of his skills with hammer and saw and decided that he could be just the man he needed. He knew that baggage handlers were not well paid, and many would be glad of earning a little extra cash in their pocket. The Craven's had decided that their new found marital happiness should be celebrated through a home make over. Their house was tired, bearing witness to two young boys. It was a home whose potential was not being fully realised. Stephen could do a lot of the work, but he would be away much of the time as his flying schedule dictated. Adele would help, but could not manage much of the heavy work, and also had the boys to look after. By now, the family were firmly established in the neighbourhood, where Adele especially had found a good circle of friends and neighbours. They thought highly of their quiet, polite and friendly neighbour, and would help out readily with the kids. But that was a part of Adele's attraction

– she was not the kind of person to take advantage of the goodwill of those around her.

What was needed to get their project completed, they both agreed, was a low-cost handyman who could do some of the grunt work, and who had the skills to assist in areas where the couple fell short. McIntire leapt at the chance.

The move appeared to be a success. The makeover was soon nearly complete, and Rusty worked so well with Adele that the two decided to set up a small decorating business. And there was the first new nail in their marital coffin. Rusty bought for Adele a cell phone and Stephen was immediately wary. The control that he needed to exert rose once more. Perhaps it was fear that he would lose his wife. Perhaps it was a perverse reaction to the guilt he felt at being away from home for long stretches at a time. Whatever, Stephen was unhappy.

It turned out that he had good cause to be. Because there was more to the relationship between Rusty and Adele than a professional, working one. The two were having an affair.

The counselling, it was clear to note, was only papering over the cracks of a breaking relationship between two unhappy people. Adele's view of the relationship is different to Rusty's, but the relationship was real. It was the extent of it that would be thrown open to doubt. Adele maintains, and stated at her trial, that the love affair was short lived. In fact, she quickly became wary of Rusty. She noted that he seemed to become obsessed by her, infatuated and it scared her.

She attempted to cool down the relationship, but Rusty had charm alongside the less desirable aspects of his personality, and she could not completely throw him off.

Rusty's account is different. He stated that the relationship with Adele was strong. But also, that, during this time, he had began drinking heavily. He was also taking an ant- depressant drug, Paxil. Like many on this medication, Rusty was keen to stop the tablets, and this would become a point that would feature heavily in the ever closer coming trial.

Meanwhile, friends of Adele reported a change in her own demeanour. The polite, cheery but quiet lady was clearly less happy. She moaned frequently about her husband, telling that she would feel happy if his plane crashed, or if she could get rid of him in some way, she would gladly do so. It seemed out of character for her to express these violent feelings, and friends knew that she was suffering some kind of distress in her life.

'Adele grew up with not a lot of money, not a lot of luxury,' said neighbour Julie Boyce. 'She was determined to make a better life.' It was clear that the better life she had carved out was not one she would readily give up.

Maybe life with Stephen was becoming unliveable but divorce might mean losing the money his job brought. Even worse, maybe her boys could be taken from her. It was too much to risk. Dr James Murray, Forensic Psychologist explained why Adele had possibly remained in her then unhappy marriage. It was not an unusual scenario. 'Women typically feel less power than men. And so, they do feel obligated in many cases to stay in relationships where they do feel threatened.

Adele was in a dilemma, and it was this that led her to make the comments about wishing her husband dead. The extent to which she meant her claims, intended to carry out her threats, is impossible to tell.

The next turn in the corkscrew of Adele's life made its indelible mark on the morning of July 12th, 2000. The mark that would be left on Stephen that day was even deeper. A mark that would be made by a combination of crowbar and bullet.

At about 9.30, Adele dropped the boys with a neighbour so that she could spend some time with Stephen and Rusty discussing the final elements of the last stages of the makeover. The basement was the final job and was almost complete. There were just some decisions to make regarding the bathroom

An hour later, Adele picked up the kids and had some errands to run, jobs which would take much of the remainder of the day. Detective Wayne Wallace, an officer on the case, picks up the story: 'They had gone to the bank, they'd gone to the cell phone store, they had gotten lunch and she'd even stopped at a neighbours' where she was going to be helping out.'

Adele did not get home with the boys, she claimed, until around 8.30pm. When she arrived, the front door was wide open. Fearing burglary, and alarmed for the safety of the boys, of Stephen and of herself, she did not enter. Instead, she popped next door to her young neighbour, Julie Boyce. Julie called her father, who went to investigate.

He scouted the house before entering, seeing if there was any evidence of a break in. It was possible, after all, that Stephen had gone out and forgotten to close the door, or perhaps even was still inside the house.

Of course, he was inside the house. He lay at the bottom of the basement stairs. Julie's father could see him, prone and surrounded by a pool of scarlet blood, as he peered in through a window at the back of the house. But so badly beaten was the body that Adele did not immediately recognise him. This might seem strange, because even in his bloodied state, the man was clothed in Stephen's attire. But equally, nor did Julie Boyce's father make an immediate identification.

The police and ambulance were called. Adele stood in a panic on the porch of the Boyce household, repeating that there was a body inside her home. But once the authorities arrived, it did not take long to fathom out the victim. It was apparent that it was Stephen Craven. And he was dead.

Detective Wayne Wallace told the Snapped investigative TV documentary the specific cause of death. 'Stephen had suffered blunt force trauma to the head. He had crow bar strikes to the forehead, to

the rear of the head and to the left and right-hand side of the head.'
He had been severely battered. But probably, it was something else that
caused the fatal injury. Stephen Craven had also been shot three times
from close range.

As is usual in circumstances such as these, despite her shock Adele
was taken in immediately for questioning. Meanwhile, the boys were
looked after by a neighbour. Adele told police, through tears and
hysteria, that it must have been a burglary that went wrong. She could
see no reason for anybody to want to murder her husband.

Yet the police had their doubts right from the start as to the
likelihood of a burglary scenario. There was a credit card and wallet,
untouched, in the office nearby. No damage had been carried out inside
the property, and nothing was obviously missing. There was no
evidence of a struggle, nor of a thief being disturbed. It looked, to
police, as though Stephen was the victim of a straightforward murder.

Yet, who would want to kill a successful airline pilot? One who
seemed to have an ideal life with a caring wife and two adoring
children? Police got their first break almost straight away. Officers at
the scene phoned their station and asked for a search on the police
database for the name Stephen Craven. Perhaps that might throw up
some unsavoury links, or evidence that the ideal life he had appeared to
lead was not as straightforward as it had seemed.

They got a shock. There were no entries for Stephen Craven. But
the name Craven was there, and it was linked to the address at which
a terrible crime had just taken place. Adele Craven was on record; her
offence was one that immediately identified her as a suspect.

Another investigator on the case, Shawn Kleier, tells the story. A
beat cop had been patrolling around the area when he was drawn to the
land behind the local church. There was a parked van, and it was pretty
obvious that something was going on inside it. When he investigated,
he found a couple engaged in public sexual activity. The woman was
Adele Craven and her partner, Rusty McIntyre.

The police investigated further and spoke to neighbours. It soon became apparent that Rusty was spending a lot of time at the Craven's home, especially when Stephen was away with his work. Aimee Boyce was a witness to this. 'I'd see him arrive at nine o clock at night, and then he'd leave the next morning.'

The net was tightening. Further investigations threw up no evidence of any suspects other than Adele and Rusty. And there was more. Police discovered a large, packed bag. Inside were clothes, including several changes of underwear belonging to Adele. Her passport and the important certifications, such as her children's birth certificates, were inside. The bag also contained $4000 in cash. It looked as though she was planning to leave. Then, a search of the cell phone Rusty had purchased for her showed hundreds of loving messages between the two, especially from him to her. The numbers ran to several calls a day. Credit card records offered further clues to illicit meetings between the two.

Police had clear evidence that Rusty McIntyre and Adele Craven were far more than just partners in business, they were sexual partners as well. Another reporter who became interested in the case, Paul Long, discovered 'They fell in love together and would meet at the Wild Wood Inn, Florence. Here they would have sex.'

It was at this point in the investigation that the police got another powerful lead as to the possibility of Adele's involvement in the crime. Aimee Boyce, the friend and neighbour, was holding on to a matter that was troubling her. Now she came forward to tell the authorities of Adele's wishes to see her husband dead; a car accident, a plane crash; it did not matter.

Soon other neighbours would tell too of similar conversations. The evidence was growing.

But it is a rare person who does not fall out with their partner. While most of us would not want that loved one dead, to say the words is not a crime. They can be exaggerations, emotional responses to a particularly bad day. Many, many people will say things that they later regret, and even when those words are as cruel as the ones uttered by Adele, there is a still an enormous gap between verbalisation and action.

Many married people become involved in affairs. We can judge the moral crime such acts commit, but there is no law against becoming involved in an extra marital affair. On the day in question, Adele had a strong alibi as to her whereabouts. None of her neighbours reported that she was in an agitated state. Police evidence consisted of nothing more than circumstances and suspicions.

But nine days after the murder, they decided to take the plunge and arrest Adele Craven for the murder of her husband. 'I found it hard to believe that Adele had anything to do with it,' said the neighbour, Aimee Boyce. They also decided to arrest Rusty, but that would prove more difficult to carry out. Because Rusty had used a sum from Adele to take his own family on a cruise. That money was the sum she had put aside to pay for a divorce from Stephen. Clearly, it was money she needed any longer. Was it a generous gift? Did she just want him out of the way for a while? However, as soon as arrived back in the States, on July 28th, police were waiting, and he too was arrested.

Adele continued to maintain her innocence of any wrong doing. She insisted that the affair with Rusty had been short lived, and that it was he who had become obsessed with her. But Rusty was not as strong. Drinking heavily, only recently having been taking anti-depressants, his own emotional state was fragile. Rusty not only confessed that he had been involved in the murder of Stephen Craven, but a third figure was now introduced into the story.

Rusty told Detective Wallace that it was not he who had carried out the crime. Nor was it Adele. In fact, he had hired another man to carry out the deed. Ronald Scott Pryor was a second-rate criminal, a crook down on his luck. Rusty told the police that he and Adele had paid to do their dirty work for them. The $15000 dollars the couple offered him was, according to officers who investigated the murder a 'huge amount of money.' He was happy to oblige.

In fact, Pryor was so desperate for money that those who were close to the case felt he would do anything for money. To him, painting a fence or clearing a back yard where no more or less worthy than killing another human. Each were jobs, each paid cash. It was just that, there was rather a lot more cash involved when the job was murder. Pryor, his greying pony tail like a greasy chain around his head, also confessed quickly.

Detective Wallace explained that there was a lot of similarity between the statements made by Rusty McIntyre and Ronald Scott. That neither of them knew the other was in custody, or had even been arrested, added weight to their conclusions that the two men, despite the horror of what they were admitting to, where telling the truth. Rusty also claimed that his decision making had been affected by the combination of coming off his anti-depressant and heavy drinking. Yes, he had been involved in the crime, yet at a time when his faculties were not functioning well.

But the quietly spoken, polite and formerly cheerful Adele held out in her story. She said that it was Rusty who had killed her husband, doing so with the mistaken idea that he could step into Stephen's place. His obsession with Adele was what drove him to organise this most terrible of crimes.

The question seemed to come down to one of two scenarios. One was true, the other a lie. Police knew the day of Stephen's death. But they did not know the time. They were sure, from neighbours and from their investigations, that Adele loved her sons too much to murder her husband, their father, in front of them. Therefore, it was the police's position that the murder took place when Adele took her sons to be looked after by neighbours, in the early part of the morning on that July day in 2000.

This was the account both Rusty and Ronald Pryor offered. They told of Stephen being led down to the basement on the pretext of discussing changes to the bathroom located there. They told of Ronald lying in wait and stepping out as Stephen reached the bottom of the stairs, there to strike at the pilot again and again with the crow bar the criminal carried.

They told of how Stephen, collapsed and bleeding heavily, still refused to die, and how Adele became increasingly frantic until in the end she handed over a handgun and Ronald Pryor shot her husband three times. Then, finally, the Delta Airlines employee succumbed and died.

Not only was this the story that both Ronald and Rusty told, independently of each other. But it also fitted with Adele's odd decision to send her children to a neighbour that morning. Looking at the bathroom should surely not have taken long, and the boys would have been safe in the house, could even have come down with the adults to the basement. Why call upon a neighbour's goodwill for such a trivial task?

But Adele told a different version of events. Her story was that the meeting over the bathroom happened as planned, and once it was over she went off to collect the boys. From there she carried out the chores she needed to complete. During this time, unbeknown to her, Rusty and Ronald had waited for their chance and killed Stephen. She had lost a husband, one with whom her relationship was beginning to recover. She had lost the father to her children.

There was circumstantial evidence in Adele's favour as well. After all, she had met a number of people during that day of small chores. And not one of those people, nor her young sons, had spotted anything unusual in her behaviour. They had not seen a woman in a panic, upset or anxious. They had not seen a woman unusually distracted. They had seen the Adele they knew and liked.

Perhaps she had blood of ice running through her veins. Anybody who planned the murder of her husband in such detail and carried it out with such callous efficiency must be a person who could control her emotions to such an extent, who could compartmentalise her feelings so effectively.

Although, of course, there could have been a very different reason for her normality that day. Adele Craven could have been innocent.

Now, though, all three faced charges of murder, a crime that carried the death penalty. Rusty McIntyre quickly did a deal whereby the capital punishment risk would be taken away if he gave evidence against the others involved and pleaded guilty himself. But Ronald Pryor, despite what he said on his arrest, changed his story. He decided to plead not guilty and withdrew his claims about Adele's involvement.

Although at his own trial Pryor was also convicted and was given the death penalty, he stuck by his determination to not implicate Adele. Luke Morgan, the assistant attorney general of the State, and also its head of special prosecutions, maintained that Pryor's change of heart was because he still had years of appeals ahead of him, and would reduce the chances of success in these if he claimed he knew of the murder and Adele was behind it. After all, he did not know Stephen Craven, so his only link to the victim was the murder itself.

But the lack of Pryor's testimony, alongside Adele's continued claim of innocence, was a problem for the prosecution. Nevertheless, she spent two years in custody, her sons given to the care of Stephen's brother, who was adamant as to his sister in law's guilt. It was a situation from which it would be hard to recover, even if she was proven to be innocent.

But within Cincinnati itself, the crime remained front page news, with interest growing exponentially as the trial approached. Such was the interest that it was decided to hold the trial eighty miles from the scene of the crime, where there was a greater chance of finding a jury who had not already made up their minds.

In court, Adele was a star witness. During her three days on the stand, she came across as a distraught, but quiet and contained, loving wife and mother. Her evidence convinced the jury. But not all of them.

After three days of deliberation eight were satisfied as to her innocence, three convinced of her guilt, and one undecided. Deadlock was reached, and neither side was prepared to step down. The judge called a mis trial, and years of stress would continue for Adele. However, generally, the result was seen as good news for the mother. The prosecution had been unable to prove her guilt. Only three jurors felt the woman from a Hispanic background was responsible for the murder of her husband.

The prosecution was worried. In all likelihood, as was normally the case in mis trials, the second court show would result in the case being thrown out. Adele would walk free. So, they devised a plan. They approached Ronald Pryor and agreed to drop the death penalty for him if he now agreed to speak against Adele. Unsurprisingly, he took the bait.

His testimony proved pivotal. With both Pryor and McIntyre speaking against her, Adele saw the way the case was going. An offer was on the table. Change your plea to guilty and the death penalty would be dropped. Life imprisonment, with a chance of parole twenty to twenty-five years on. The offer was too good, and Adele changed her stance, and admitted to the crime. Her supporters maintained she had little choice.

So now she sits in a Kentucky penitentiary. Whether she is a woman wrongly convicted, forced to choose the best of bad options, or whether she is a woman who planned the murder of her husband, dragging two others into her crime is something we will probably never know for sure.

COLD BLOODED KILLER CHRISTINA WALTERS

15

JENNIFER MARTIN

Christina "Shea" Walters: Cold Blooded Killer or Victim of Circumstance?

The Crime

It was a typical, hot August North Carolina night on August 17, 1998. Eighteen-year-old Tracy Lambert and her twenty-one-year-old friend, Susan Moore, were planning a night out on the town. The two vibrant, young blondes did their hair and make-up together and made plans to meet with friends. They got into Moore's car, and headed out toward their meeting place.

Suddenly, they were being tailed by an angry group of young strangers. The strangers were waving guns out the window, flashing their headlights, and yelling. Moore attempted to flee the group, but in a moment of terrified disorientation, she pulled down a dead-end road. Three young men approached the vehicle with guns drawn and forced the women into the trunk of Moore's car. The vehicle began moving with one of the young men behind the steering wheel. When it stopped, the men opened the trunk and demanded the women hand over their jewelry. Once all the jewelry was taken from the women, the trunk was again closed and the car began moving once again.

The second time the car stopped, the trunk was opened to reveal a larger group against the back drop of a trailer park. The group began discussing how to "dispose" of the women, causing Lambert to cry out and plead for mercy. A young American Indian woman expressed disgust with Lambert's "pathetic whimpering," and slammed the trunk door back shut. The men piled back into Moore's car while the rest of the group got into a second vehicle. The cars followed one another into an open, rural area where Lambert and Moore were forced out of the car. Each of the women was dragged into the open by one of the men who had committed the carjacking. Moore began pleading for their lives. She reportedly asked the men, "What are you going to do to us? Are you going to kill us?" She followed the question by trying to compromise, stating, "We don't know what you look like. Just let us go." At that point, one man held a gun to Tracy Lambert's head and said, "Well, I'm about to open this bitch's third eye." Lambert then started crying and said, "Oh, my god, Susan. We're going to die. We're going to die. I don't want to die." The gunman then told Tracy to "Shut up" before shooting her in the head. Another man was holding onto Moore with a knife to her throat as she watched her friend be killed. She began sobbing and begged him not to cut her throat, offering to him that he could just shoot her, instead. He showed mercy in that one small instance and borrowed the gun from his friend, ending her life instantly.

By midnight, friends and family were already concerned that the women had not arrived at the social gathering and began to look. An anonymous phone call alerted the police that the caller had "seen some people get shot." Sometime around dawn, the bodies were reported as discovered.

Earlier that same night, Debra Cheeseborough was leaving work at Bojangles when a young man, his face hidden beneath a bandana, approached her, placed a gun to her side, and told her if she'd cooperate, he would not hurt her. He ordered her into the trunk of her own car, where she lay still, quietly praying as a group of young people, all unidentifiable beneath their bandana masks, climbed into her car and began driving. Presumably as they dug through the contents of her purse and glove box, one of the young men came to the realization that he had gone to school with Debra's daughter.

Debra felt a glimmer of hope in that instant. She thought that, maybe, because they had made a connection, they would let her go without harming her. That hope was crushed when she heard the young people joking about how they had disliked her daughter and how much fun it was going to be to get rid of her mother.

The group pulled the car into an isolated area of Fort Bragg and ordered Debra from the trunk. She cried and pleaded for her life to no avail. Several of the young people, each with their own gun, began firing bullets into her. She was shot all over her body until the group was confident that she was dead. They left her lying on the ground and drove away in her car.

Debra later testified that, as she laid in the field, she could hear the voice of her deceased mother comforting her. "She told me it wasn't my time yet," she said under oath. "She told me she was going to help me get to the road, but not too close where someone could hit me." Debra did manage to drag herself to the roadside, where she was spotted by a passing motorist. She survived her injuries that night and went on to testify against her attackers in court, ultimately putting many of them away for life.

The night of August 17, 1998 was, no doubt, life altering for all parties involved in the events that unfolded in Fayetteville, North Carolina. This included twenty-year-old Christina "Shea" Walter. On the night of the crime spree, Christina had gathered at her trailer home at 1386 Davis Street in Fayetteville along with friends Francisco Tirado, Eric Queen, John Juarbe, Tameika Douglas, Ione Black, Carlos Nevills, Darryl Tucker, and Carlos Frink. Having grown up on the "wrong side of the tracks," all nine of the young people who gathered at the trailer had aligned themselves with the "Crip" gang, although they each claimed different "sets" or subgroups of the gang. The subgroups had come together and realized that the gang, as a whole, was in need of money. They formulated a plan to steal a car and drive it through the front window of a pawn shop, where they would steal the inventory.

Earlier in the afternoon, the nine friends had gone to Wal-Mart. They bought bullets with which they were going to carry out their plan and stole clothing and toiletries. When they arrived back at the trailer,

Tirado borrowed Christina's blue fingernail polish to color the tips of the bullets blue. This was symbolic, the group agreed, of the "Crips" gang.

After discussing their plan, the group split up. Christina, Douglas, Nevills, and Black called a friend to drive them into a quiet neighborhood. Christina gave Nevills a gun and told him to find a victim and put them in the trunk of a car, then return to her trailer within an hour and a half.

Debra Cheeseborough was their first victim.

After the group thought they had killed Cheeseborough, they returned to Christina's trailer where they discussed their plan further. They realized that they needed another car. Christina, Tucker, Black, and Queen took Cheeseborough's car in search of another victim, ultimately finding Tracy Lambert and Susan Moore.

After killing the two young women, the group decided to call it a night and meet up at the trailer the next day. However, Tirado had trouble sleeping and kept one ear to the police scanner all night. At around dawn, he called Christina and reported to her that bodies had been found. From there, the entire group, with the exception of Black and Nevills, fled to Myrtle beach in Cheeseborough and Moore's cars, using her cell phone to place calls back to family and friends.

On Tuesday, August 18th, police in Myrtle Beach arrested Juarbe and Tucker and impounded Cheeseborough's car. The next day, they received an anonymous tip that Christina had rented a room at the Bona Villa motel in Myrtle Beach. They checked out the tip and found Moore's car in the parking lot. There, they apprehended Christina, Frink, Douglas, Queen, and Tirado. Soon, there was a media frenzy.

The Outcry

Throughout Fayetteville, the deaths of Lambert & Moore and the brutally savage attack on Debra Cheeseborough left the community enraged. The news that the crime spree was related to gang activity created a frenzy of individuals calling to "clean up the streets." News outlets flashed pictures of Moore and Lambert, two white, blonde haired, beautiful young ladies, but were less inclined to show images of Debra Cheeseborough, a middle-aged black woman. This, according to the defense, fed into a racial divide. Without knowing that Cheeseborough was a minority woman, herself, many within Fayetteville believed the violence was a hate crime against white people, instigated by a violent gang of minority youths. The fact that the attacks had been random was lost in the coverage and, soon, Fayetteville found itself in the throes of racial and economic divide.

The Woman

Not much is known about Christina's life before the events that unfolded that fateful night in 1998. Based on statements presented to her attorney, we can surmise that Christina's upbringing was less than ideal. She has made claims of being abused physically, emotionally, and sexually as a child. In one story, which would later come back to haunt her during trial, she spoke of cutting a man with a box cutter as he was trying to sexually abuse her.

As is the case with a lot of youths who feel displaced from their families and communities, Christina sought the embrace of whatever makeshift form of family she could find. In her case, she fell into a crowd of similarly dysfunctional minority youths who claimed membership to one of the largest street gangs in America: The Crips.

As Christina reached adulthood, she was able to secure her own place to live, which opened up a meeting ground for herself and fellow gang members to congregate in. Because her home was often the meeting point, she found herself in the position of leader and would often have to assert her dominance over other gang members who tried to challenge her. There is little doubt that the control Christina found within the gang was a welcome change from her helpless childhood. Christina no doubt realized that, in her newly given position, she could find safety in her power. She became a fearless leader of her group and was unafraid to assert herself with dominance or even threats of death.

Until that August night, though, Christina had never actually killed anyone. As would be explained in court by her co-defendants, to kill someone for the good of the gang is one of the highest honors the Crips had established at the time. The honor was memorialized with a teardrop tattoo on the face following a "confirmed kill."

Christina saw the carjacking plan as an opportunity to earn the highest honor she could for her gang, securing herself a position of leadership for life. To those of us who have grown up in more mild environments, it seems to be an act of selfishness and a fool's errand. To Christina, though, it would mean a lifetime of security from anyone that would ever attempt to cause her pain.

As the gang made plans to secure funds for their needs, Christina made plans of her own.

As the events unfolded, Christina remained mostly quiet about her intent to kill the carjacking victims. As each of the cars were stolen, the women were brought back to Christina's trailer to discuss their fates. It was only then that Christina expressed her desire for the women to be killed.

To refuse to kill someone for the benefit of the gang would have been suicide. With no other option but to help Christina, the co-defendants carried out Christina's plan alongside her. Because they had done so, Christina was responsible for helping them attempt to escape punishment, which is why she paid the way for everyone to go to Myrtle Beach.

Some of Christina's supporters today make a case that Christina wasn't cold-blooded. She was simply living the only life she knew how to survive in, and that her case was unnecessarily worsened by the media attention and dishonesty of news outlets at the time. Rumors regarding Christina's character and the lifestyle of the gang itself began to circulate. Soon enough, the story had evolved into a tale that Christina forced the co-defendants to kill two white women as a form of initiation into the gang. This was simply not the truth, but it was a tale that the defense had trouble running from. In the end, Christina "Shea" Walters believed the rumors and unfair media exposure were responsible for the severity of her sentencing.

The Trial

Regardless of Christina's culpability, she suffered from having inadequate representation at her trial. She was advised that, because of the media attention surrounding the case, the courts would issue a change of venue and try her somewhere other than Fayetteville. Unbeknownst to her, she would have had to file a motion for the change of venue. By the time she realized the need for her to initiate the motion, it was too late to file and her case was stuck at the center of a media whirlwind.

Because of the public nature of the case, Christina believes she was unable to receive a fair trial. According to her defense, eight of the twelve jurors that were seated on the jury had already been informed of the details of her case by other potential jurors and courtroom staff prior to the trial beginning. The state of North Carolina rebutted this claim stating that each juror swore to be fair and impartial and to disregard any information they had heard or read prior to the beginning of the proceedings. The state also argues that Christina never objected to the jurors at the appropriate time when she should have. Christina argues that, again, her defense team failed her and she did not know her rights.

She also claims she did not know her rights when she failed to file a motion for the murders of Lambert and Moore to be tried separately from the attack on Cheeseborough. Trying the crimes at the same time, she says, is partly to blame for the outcome of the proceedings.

Probably one of Christina's most compelling arguments that she did not receive a fair trial, however, comes with evidence logged right into the court report, itself. During the selection of the jurors, the Judge actually left the court room. During that time, a reporter began interviewing a potential juror about the case. The transcript reads as follows;

Judge: And, Madam Clerk, would you go ahead and call another juror please for number five?

Clerk: Richard Council.

Judge: Thank you. Counsel, I have to make a phone call to my district attorney. If you'll give me just a moment, please? (Leaves courtroom)

(Number five, Mr. Council, enters court room.)

Bailiff: Sir, come on up and have a seat in number five.

(A male media representative was talking to the juror, Mr. Council, as the juror walked by.)

Court Reporter: Tell that guy to quit talking to the juror- that media guy.

(Bailiff, Sgt. David Farrell, directed number five, Mr. Council, in the box after Sgt. Farrell spoke to the media representative.)

(Judge returns to courtroom.)

Judge: Remain seated.

Bailiff: Come to order. Court's in session.

Christina argues that, because the media had time to address the juror, and because nobody in the court room bothered to inform the Judge of the interaction, the juror was tampered with prior to the beginning of the proceedings and had already been given an "insider's idea" of what the hope of the community was for the outcome of her case.

Finally, Christina says that her past was brought up in court unnecessarily, with facts "twisted" to make her seem like a more brutal and violent person than she really believes herself to be. This is where the case falls back to the instance of self- defense against a sexual predator. Again, the evidence is in the transcript:

Prosecutor: Did you say your dad almost killed a boy that you stabbed?

Christina: I haven't stabbed no boy.

Prosecutor: Did you say that?

Christina: No, ma'am. I don't remember saying anything like that.

Prosecutor: Do you remember saying the boy you stabbed was 20-something at the time?

Christina: Unless the person who wrote this was talking about when I had a boyfriend who was trying to take my shirt off and I sliced him with a box cutter, but that's not stabbing.

At this point in the trial, the Judge did excuse the jury momentarily to ask the prosecutor why they were asking these questions. During the conversation, the Judge asked the defense why he had not objected to the questioning, clearly recognizing that it was a bad direction for the defense to allow the questioning to go.

Failing Christina, yet again, the defense attorney responded, "Well, because we didn't care at the point she was at."

One has to wonder- if a judge sees a line of questioning that is so outrageous he will dismiss the jury and ask, himself, why nobody is objecting to it- how does the defense, itself, not recognize the issue? Christina's supporters say that she was being defended by a court-appointed attorney who, they claim, was already swayed by the media outcry against Christina. He did not wish for her to win her case, so he did not even try to offer her a solid defense.

During the same testimony, Christina admitted that she shot several .32 caliber bullets into Cheeseborough, only stopping once she thought the victim was dead. Cheeseborough was able to testify against Walters, although she stated in her testimony that she could not positively identify her shooters. In appeals, Christina has stated that she was not well- advised by her attorney and only confessed to attempting to kill Cheeseborough because she believed that, because the victim of her shooting had survived, she would not be tied to the deaths of the other two women.

His failure to object to the unfair questioning, compiled with his failure to alert the judge of the jury tampering and not clearly outlining

Christina's rights to her prior to trial are all signs indicating that, perhaps, Christina and her followers may be correct in their assumption.

In July of 2000, the trial came to a close with Christina Walters sentenced to Death. Eric Queen and Paco Tirado were both also sentenced to death in the months prior. With the ruling, Christina became the fifth woman on North Carolina's death row and secured herself a place as one of the state's most notorious female killers.

While there is little doubt that the acts committed against Tracy Lambert, Susan Moore, and Debra Cheeseborough on that August night were horrendous and cruel, there is reason to question whether or not Walters received a fair trial and sentencing in accordance with her legal rights under Federal law. Around the country, as news of the court case spread, Walters acquired supporters who felt empathy for her unfortunate upbringing and believed that she had been "railroaded" in court. As her following grew, the case began receiving attention from a new light, ultimately leading to a re-examination of the facts.

The Commuted Sentence

In December of 2012, a North Carolina judge commuted Christina Walters's death sentence along with the death sentences of two other convicted killers as part of the scaling back of the Racial Justice Act. The decision in each of the three cases came after a four-week deliberation on their individual cases in which the prosecution was proven to have made a conscious and indisputable error to reduce the number of black jurors in the original trials.

Although each of the prosecutors argued that they had, in fact, not made any such effort, the judge said that it was ultimately their own mannerisms and testimony that proved otherwise. "The conclusion is based primarily on the words and deeds of prosecutors involved in these cases," he said. "Despite presentations to the contrary, their words, their deeds, speak volumes. During presentation of evidence, the court finds powerful and persuasive evidence of racial consciousness, race-based decision making in the writings of prosecutors long buried in the case files and brought to light for the first time during this hearing."

Christina Walters, a Lumbee Indian, having been proven to have been tried unfairly based on her race, was commuted from death row to a life sentence without the possibility of parole.

The Repeal

In December of 2015, the Supreme Court vacated the commute claiming that the Judge did not give prosecutors adequate time to respond to a statistical study on race in the North Carolina state court system. The Racial Justice Act was also overturned, causing Christina Walters to, once again, have to appeal her case.

The study referenced concluded in 2011 showed that racial bias played a role in culling jurors before death penalty trials. Prosecutors disagreed with the claims, stating that the race of the juror doesn't play a role in their decision for keeping or releasing someone from the jury selection panel. The study examined 173 capital trials over a 20-year period to accumulate evidence to the contrary.

Qualified black jurors were over twice as likely to be released from panels under peremptory strikes according to Michigan State University's study of capital cases ranging from 1990 to 2010. Prosecutors argued that the study was invalid because the range of statistics stretched out far too broadly, failing to present an accurate depiction of how jurors are currently selected.

The Supreme Court encouraged both sides to prevent additional studies to support their claims.

In January of 2017, Christina Walters's legal team appealed her death sentence by using the now-repealed Racial Justice Act. Prosecutors argued that she couldn't use the repealed act because it has been repealed. Her defense argued that she had obtained relief under the Act and that it was unfair to strip her of that relief retroactively.

Judge Spainhour from Raleigh, North Carola presided over the case. He decided that Christina Walters's case was still pending under the Racial Justice Act and, therefore she could no longer use the repealed act.

There is little doubt that Christina Walters and her supporters will continue to appeal their case in pursuit of a commuted sentence or a retrial. With the buzz surrounding the case, it's hard not to look at the entirety of the situation objectively to determine if Christina is really the cold and calculated killer that prosecution in the original trial portrayed her to be or if, instead, she is a young woman led astray by circumstance, then railroaded by a court system designed to work against her.

Jay Ferguson, an attorney on her legal team, was quoted in the Fayetteville News Observer as saying, "We are confident that, no matter how many hearings are held or studies completed, we will win this case. The evidence of racial bias in jury selection is simply overwhelming and undeniable. All this decision will do is add more delays and cost the state millions to conduct new studies and hold new hearings. We will be throwing more taxpayer money into a hopelessly broken death penalty."

SERIAL KILLER DOCTOR : THE TRUE STORY OF ALICE WYNEKOOP

NATHAN NIXON

The Wynekoop Case

There are few murder cases in history that have been as bizarre as The Wynekoop case. Perhaps it is the circumstance of a mother allegedly committing an awful act for her son that grabbed so much attention. Maybe it was the sense among American's that such a seemingly sweet and noble woman could not possibly have committed such a crime. During a time in the United States that is already a tale of struggle and recovery, this murder set in 1933 stood in the headlines for weeks and gripped an entire class of people along the way. The story of Dr. Alice L. Wynekoop is one for the ages.

Alice Lindsay was born in 1870. Although little was recorded or known of her early life, it is well documented that she lived an absolutely normal childhood. The importance of The Wynekoop case begins with her marriage to Frank Wynekoop in the 1890's. Alice Lindsay took the famous name, now, of Alice Lindsay Wynekoop. She worked hard in her education in the medical field, and soon became a full practicing doctor in the late 1890's. By the turn of the century, Dr. Alice Wynekoop, along with her husband Frank Wynekoop, would start to put together the foundation for what would later become one of the Chicago area's most chilling scenes.

The beginning of this chilling case actually begins in 1901. Frank and Alice Wynekoop decided to supervise the construction of a massive red-bricked mansion in the west side of Chicago. Their thinking was to create a safe, family centered environment for their entire family. Soon after, the property was popularly said to be "cursed". Frank and Alice had several children. Their daughter, Marie Louise, died there inside the home in an upstairs bedroom. Frank's brother, Dr. Gilbert Wynekoop, put the entire family in the headlines when he attempted to strangle his unfaithful wife during their divorce proceedings. This was said to have happened in the family living room. Dr. Gilbert Wynekoop later was clinically diagnosed as insane and was institutionalized.

All of these dreadful event happened in a 20 year timespan leading up to the dreariest event of them all. Before the murder, the house was already tagged as haunted throughout the neighborhood. The Wynekoop's were ultimately the black sheep of the neighborhood. It is important to keep in mind the era that this is in. This was a time in American History when the totality of medical care was transitioning to major hospitals and medical establishments. There was still, however, significant medical care that was happening in local housing. The Wynekoop household fit this bill. They had several rooms in the house devoted to the family medical practice. There were rooms for operations and general care as well as a morgue in the basement. This was obviously well known in the neighborhood, and gave more material for the whispers around town to gossip about. Those whispers gained a much bigger voice in 1933.

Prior to 1933, there was actually some positivity toward Dr. Alice Wynekoop. While many spoke of the property being haunted and many in the neighborhood holding a genuine fear of going around the house, that opinion was not generally shared in regards to Frank and Alice Wynekoop. Dr. Alice Wynekoop was an influential figure in the women's suffrage movement as well as an advocate for women's rights as a whole. Alice graduated medical school from Northwestern University in Illinois. She was generally admired and held in high regard for her medical practicing in the area. She would commonly provide medical care to those in need when they may not have had the means to garner medical attention from other places. She was a one of the primary leaders in the evolution of child healthcare and believed wholeheartedly in fair, honest medical treatment of everyone, regardless of their income or ability to pay. For these reasons, the bizarre events of 1933 still have people split on what really happened. Dr. Alice Wynekoop, for all intents and purposes, could also be called a killer and a liar.

The relationship that Alice had with her son is of supreme importance to the case. Frank and Alice's son, Earle Wynekoop, was generally described as a low-life. Specifically, he desired to stay in the mansion as long as possible. He often leeched money off of Alice and Frank and was never really forced to grow up.

In 1929, Dr. Frank Wynekoop, the husband of Alice Wynekoop, passed away. This left the massive 16 bedroom mansion with only Alice Wynekoop, Earle Wynekoop, and Rheta Wynekoop, the wife of Earle.

Earle and Rheta Wynekoop had an unsuccessful marriage to say the least. After her death, a deep investigation was conducted by investigators into the past of Earle Wynekoop. Earle was said to have a "black book" with as many as 50 names in it. He frequented fairs, where he would set out to woo as many women as he could. He famously is said to have had "as many as 25 fiancée's" at one point in time. Many women who would later be questioned said that "he made love to them in the strangest and most repulsive ways." This would all lead to Rheta Wynekoop questioning their marriage. Rheta grew tremendously depressed and often times found herself in competition with Earle's lovers. She famously weighed herself as much as ten times per day.

Although Earle had fallen out of love with Rheta shortly after their honeymoon, the marriage continued in the oddest of circumstances. In 1933, the Wynekoop mansion housed Alice, Earle, Rheta, and a boarder or little significance to the case. The basement of the mansion was the site of great medical care as well as several other bedrooms in the house. This was an odd living situation for all involved.

Dr. Alice Wynekoop tried all that she could to support the marriage. Strangely enough, this repulsed Rheta even more. Rheta felt that Alice had "blind support" for Earle, regardless of what he did and how he did it. To supremely set the stage for baffling case, Alice had taken up life insurance policies on Rheta just weeks before her tragic death. Upon the death of Rheta Wynekoop, Alice was set to collect

$12,000, a staggering amount of money in the depression era in the early 1930's.

The overall situation of the Wynekoop's was a bit strange. With all of these things considered, it is no wonder how there could be reasonable suspicion raised about Dr. Wynekoop's part in a heinous crime. The events of the murder are both chilling and confusing. The night of November 21, 1933 will forever be an event that still has many questions surrounding it.

The Murder

It was around 10 P.M. that a police officer that was out on patrol was dispatched to the Wynekoop home. Who was the person who phoned police on that evening? Ironically enough, the caller was none other than Dr. Alice Wynekoop.

"Something terrible has happened," Dr. Alice Wynekoop said to police upon entering the home. "Come on downstairs and I will show you."

Officers would describe Alice Wynekoop as anxious and jittery. The officer notably referenced a calm in her voice, however.

The group made their way downstairs to the doctor's operating room in the Wynekoop home. Immediately upon entering the room, it was quickly clear that something wasn't quite right.

On a table in the center of the room lay a body. The body was still slightly warm to the touch and showed evidence of very recent death. A sheet had been thrown over the body, leaving only bare feet and the head and upper shoulders exposed. The face had numerous scratches on it, however nothing specifically deep or significant. There was moderate bruising over many parts of the body as well as discoloration on several areas of the flesh. It appeared as if there was some sort of struggle that took place before the body was placed on the table. This was the body of Rheta Wynekoop, wife of Earle Wynekoop and daughter in law off Dr. Alice Wynekoop.

Upon further examination of the body, it was quickly discovered that Rheta had suffered a gunshot wound through the back. With closer examination, the bullet was tracked to have entered the back just above the midline and to have taken an upward course through the torso. The bullet was lodged just beneath Rheta's left breast. After autopsy, the final exam would show that the entire thorax was filled with blood. The overall significance to investigators with this information was that it showed Rheta was alive when she was shot. This indicated that the official cause of death was the gunshot wound to her back causing hemorrhage and shock. The manner of death was officially ruled a homicide.

Autopsy also revealed a significant level of chloroform. Chloroform held many important medicinal uses, especially in the 1930's. A common anesthetic, chloroform was a popular choice among doctors as an agent to administer prior to a surgery. Investigation of the scene found a bottle of chloroform in the operatory room where Rheta was found. It was almost completely empty.

Also found at the crime scene was a revolver. The revolver showed signs that it had just been fired. There were also three displaced cartridges next to the revolver. This would prove to be the murder weapon. Oddly enough, the revolver belonged to Earle Wynekoop.

Earle Wynekoop would seem to have been a prime suspect upon the initial discovery of the body of Rheta. After all, he was in a marriage that he had no interest in being in. He had countless instances of unfaithfulness to support this theory. Rheta was unhappy with the marriage as well, as she knew of his acts outside of their marriage.

Earle Wynekoop was not at the house at the time of the murder according the Dr. Alice Wynekoop and others at the scene. Police questioned Earle and this statement was supported. Earle Wynekoop was driving to Arizona at the time of the murder. This led investigators to quickly eliminate him as a suspect in the murder. Dr. Wynekoop's daughter did not live in the house hold. She was a physician at Cook County Hospital. While Dr. Alice Wynekoop's daughter was present at the home at the time of the murder, it was professed to authorities by Alice Wynekoop that she was only asked for help after the body was discovered. Enid Hennessey, who was renting out a room at the house, was not accounted for at the time of the murder. She was quickly ruled out as a suspect as she had no connection to the family nor the murder beyond maintaining a temporary living arrangement.

This left only Dr. Alice Wynekoop as a suspect. Police initially marked her as the prime suspect being as she apparently identified the body first. According to Alice's initial information that she gave to police on scene, the other members of the household had no contact with Rheta and couldn't have possibly been involved.

Police quickly got a statement from Alice Wynekoop as to what happened that evening. This is truly where things get complicated in this case. Dr. Alice Wynekoop's first statement was, perhaps, a far-fetched effort to lead investigator's down a winding road that could not necessarily be disproven.

According to the first statement, Dr. Alice Wynekoop entered the operatory at precisely 8:30 P.M. to "obtain some medicine for flu-like symptoms for both her and Enid." As she arrived in the room, she saw Rheta lying on the table. Alice examined her and confirmed that she was dead. It was at this time that Dr. Alice Wynekoop called her daughter at the hospital and notified her of what happened. Catherine Wynekoop quickly came home from the hospital and pronounced Rheta dead.

It was at this time that a red flag was apparent to investigators. Rather than immediately notify police of what happened, Dr. Alice Wynekoop instead chose to call an undertaker.

Alice Wynekoop was questioned as to who could have committed this murder if all was true as she said. Dr. Wynekoop blamed the murder on thieves. She explained that there had been numerous instances that her home was broken into by thieves who were out to collect money and drugs from her operating rooms down stairs.

Police found this all to be quite misleading. If she indeed suspected that Rheta had been murdered by thieves in an apparent break in, why would she not call authorities upon discovering Rheta's body?

The deck was beginning to stack against Dr. Wynekoop. Police questioned her a second time a few days later. She gave a nearly identical statement that featured even more details of how she discovered the body. She attempted to explain to authorities that even if she had notified authorities, Rheta was already dead when she found her. This still, however, baffled police. Moreover, extensive crime scene investigation of all of the downstairs offices of the Wynekoop home showed that there was no evidence of a burglary and there was nothing that was missing to provide evidence of a burglary. This left everything pointing still toward Dr. Alice Wynekoop as the murderer of Rheta Wynekoop.

For all of these extensive reasons, police arrested Dr. Alice Wynekoop and charged her with the murder of her daughter-in-law, Rheta Wynekoop. It was at this time that Alice gave the chilling statement that would be used at trial. The statement she would give was a completely irrational argument that defied belief. This third official statement has long been seen as one of the most erratic and random stories to explain a crime in recent history.

Dr. Alice Wynekoop would go into detail about some of the habits of Rheta.

"Rheta was greatly concerned about her health and her overall appearance," Alice said in her statement. "She was always weighing herself, usually stripping down to the nude in order to do so. On Tuesday, November 21, after a luncheon, at about 1:00 P.M. she decided to go into town to buy some sheet music that she had long been wanting."

Police immediately knew that this was going to work its way into a confession. The statement was carefully taken. It was during the opening parts of her confession that police noticed that her story was already changing dramatically from anything she had stated before.

"Rheta had decided to weigh herself before she headed into town. I was working in the operatory. She was sitting on the table, practically naked. She complained that she had pain in her side that was causing much more trouble than usual. I remarked to her that since it was a convenient time during the month for an examination of this kind, we should just as well conduct it."

"She was complaining of considerable pain and tenderness throughout the beginning of the examination," Wynekoop said.

It was at this time that the initial problem began according to Dr. Alice Wynekoop. Alice stated that she suggested some Chloroform be used to make the exam go easier. Dr. Wynekoop then prepared a Chloroform solution that Rheta self-administered using a medicinal sponge.

"She took several deep, slow inhalations of the sponge," Wynekoop said. "I continued my exam and asked her if I was hurting her. She gave no answer."

Dr. Alice Wynekoop continued with her confession. She admitted that when Rheta failed to provide any sort of answer after the Chloroform had been given, she examined her at once. She determined that her breathing had stopped. She administered CPR and artificial respiration techniques immediately for roughly 20 minutes, with no success. Alice Wynekoop examined her fully with a stethoscope, and no heartbeat was revealed. For all intents and purposes, she was officially dead at this point.

The next part of the confession is where things get extremely complicated. At this point in the confession, investigators tend to think that this could be a reasonable instance of doctor error. Assuming what she was confessing at this point were true, she could realistically have been charged with negligent manslaughter. It was what she would continue on to say that baffled investigators and opened the door for conspiracy theories by many.

"I wondered what action could best ease the situation for everyone involved," Dr. Alice Wynekoop went on to confess. "The presence of a loaded revolver seemed to offer the answers that I was seeking. Further injury was now impossible. With great difficulty, I exploded one cartridge at a distance of some half dozen inches from the patient. The gun dropped from my hand."

"The scene was so overwhelming. No action was possible for a period of several hours," She continued.

With this confession, police had all of the evidence that they needed to charge and convict their prime suspect of first-degree murder. Prosecutors were able to use this third statement as confession and admit it to the court room during trial. Although there were many questions that were unanswered, the jury quickly found Dr. Alice Wynekoop guilty of first-degree murder. She was sentenced to 25 years in prison. Being as how she was 62 years old at the time of conviction, this sentence basically was a life sentence.

Assuming that the confession given by Dr. Alice Wynekoop were true, it left a mess of unanswered questions that the defense team tried to use in the court room.

The most pressing question was an obvious one. Alice Wynekoop admitted to firing the shot that killed Rheta Wynekoop. The issue with this is, however, is that she admitted to only one shot. There were three displaced cartridges at the murder scene. The mystery surrounding the other two shots has long been unsolved, as only one bullet was confirmed to have entered into Rheta's body. Many suggest that perhaps Dr. Alice Wynekoop was set to commit suicide, but couldn't keep the gun nestled out of fear. This is just a theory obviously, but no real answer has ever come about.

When police initially came to discover the body of Rheta Wynekoop, it was noted that she had significant amounts of bruising on her body. The bruising was not isolated to one spot. There was discoloration noted on numerous parts of her body. Along with bruising and discoloration were scratches. There were several noticeable scratches to her face and neck area. There wasn't a single part of Dr. Alice Wynekoop's confession that explained these marks. There was no part of the confession that talked of even the slightest struggle. This has long led many to speculate that Rheta was never murdered in the operatory room. A wide belief by many is that the murder happened elsewhere outside of the home. Chloroform was used to make her lose consciousness and she was later shot to finish the job. The bruising and scratches would be evidence that there was a struggle to get her to inhale the Chloroform. The further bruising would show signs of the unconscious body being moved from several locations. This has widely been an accepted theory, especially by those who believe that Earle Wynekoop was really the murderer.

Many wondered what would push an otherwise rational, humanely practicing doctor to commit such a heartless, inhumane act. Police admittedly were shocked at the confession and wondered how she could have gotten to this point. Perhaps the most widely accepted conspiracy theory that has come about with this case is the mother-son conspiracy. This theory is based off of the thought that Dr. Alice Wynekoop could not have possibly committed such a heinous crime. This theory goes into detail about how Earle Wynekoop was stuck in a marriage that was only bringing him misery. Earle also was vastly unsuccessful and freeloading off of his mother. After pressure from both Rheta and his mother, he was at his end with the pressure of it all.

The theory goes to say that Earle Wynekoop shot Rheta Wynekoop in the back outside of the home. He then loaded her body into his car and took her to the Wynekoop home. Upon getting the body into the operatory room, Dr. Alice Wynekoop determined her to be dead. Alice

Wynekoop had an unbreakable love for her son. She quickly came up with a plan to take blame for the murder so that her son would not get in trouble. Earle Wynekoop was then told by Alice to get in the car and start driving before she called to notify police. This would give him an alibi. It was now that she tried to frame herself for the murder and planned her story.

While there are several details added and taken away depending on who you are hearing this theory from, the basis of it is a simple concept. In criminal history, this sort of murder that the theory suggest is quite common. Essentially, a husband or wife wants out of a marriage. To them, murder is an option to get out of the marriage and save reputation and money.

To take this theory even a bit further, many suggest that perhaps Earle and Alice even planned the murder. This is how some explain Dr. Alice Wynekoop taking out the life insurance policy on Rheta for $12,000. While the defense team argues that this is merely a coincidence, it is hard to ignore the timing of that with the murder.

Yet another detail from the confession that didn't make any sense to investigators was the cause of death. Dr. Alice Wynekoop confessed that the Chloroform was what, in fact, killed Rheta Wynekoop. She admitted that she shot Rheta in the back only after she was dead in an effort to perhaps escape persecution. This in itself doesn't make much sense, but when this is coupled with the coroner's report, is just plain false. The blood found in the thorax of Rheta Wynekoop proves that she was alive when she was shot in the back. This is another red flag that many see as more evidence that points to Alice Wynekoop making up a story to cover for someone.

There has also been shaky evidence of the exact whereabouts of Earle Wynekoop on the day of the murder. While Alice Wynekoop stated that he had left on Sunday for his business trip to Arizona, it was confirmed by Stanley Young of Chicago, a nephew of E. Q. Johnson, former United States District Attorney, that Earle and Alice

Wynekoop had a secret meeting on Tuesday morning at 8:00 A.M. This is considered highly odd in any circumstance. Moreover, it is incredibly suspicious that Earle Wynekoop was emphatic about not notifying Rheta that he was still in Chicago.

Stanley Young confirmed that Earle was in Chicago on the day of the murder. While Earle would soon be on the road on the day of the murder, this makes it entirely feasible that something could have happened that morning and he left town to gain an alibi by the time the crime was reported.

Throughout this entire case, police felt like things just didn't add up. Initially, they felt like they had their suspect in Dr. Alice Wynekoop. When Alice Wynekoop ultimately confessed to the entire thing, things still just didn't quite add up to all involved.

Typically, an investigation is centered on the testimony of a suspect who is trying to prove their innocence. The suspect will contort the truth and tell a fabricated statement in a way that will prove they had nothing to do with the crime. Most often, these false statements are quickly picked through by investigators and the truth comes to the surface based on hard evidence and the work of many. This case, however, seems like the opposite happened. Years later, it became more apparent that Dr. Alice Wynekoop was likely not the murderer of Rheta Wynekoop. The puzzling part of the entire case though is that she seemingly lied and fabricated a story in an effort to be found guilty. While everyone could see the obvious flaw in her testimony, she put herself in a position to be found guilty. Whatever really happened on November 21, 1933 in that Chicago neighborhood will never actually be known. This will always be remembered as a case that found the guilty seemingly lying to go to jail.

The Crimes of The Papin Sisters

Amy Delaney

The Papin Sisters

Clémence Derré did not have the best reputation. She was well known for being promiscuous and was not a desirable candidate for Gustave Papin, whose parents disliked the girl, especially after finding out about her affair with her boss. She was the talk of the town, but Gustave was in love, and nothing anybody else could say or do would change his mind. Besides which, Clémence was pregnant with Gustave's baby, and Gustave wanted to do the right thing.

On October 3rd, 1901, Gustave Papin and Clémence Derré were married, and four months later on February 12th, 1902, their daughter Emilia was born.

However, things did not go the way Gustave had imagined. His young wife had absolutely no interest in either her new daughter, or in fact, her husband, and showed little affection to either.

Gustave's suspicions began to grow. Having steadfastly stood by Clémence when the town people had turned against her, he now began to believe that maybe the rumours had been true after all. He started to wonder if it was possible that his wife had not only had an affair with her boss but was still doing so.

Gustave made several attempts to catch his wife out – lying in wait whenever and wherever he thought they might be, but his efforts proved futile.

With his jealousy growing, Gustave decided that the only solution would be to move his wife and daughter away from the town altogether, taking Clémence out of temptation's way.

Gustave set about turning his plans into reality, and in July 1904 he secured himself a position at a saw mill in Marigné, 8km away, believing it to be a second chance for the couple. However, Clémence was furious – she had no desire to leave her home or her lover and reacted by threatening suicide. But by this time she was pregnant with the couple's second child, so she resigned herself to starting a new life in a new village, knowing that nobody else would want a pregnant woman.

On March 8th, 1905, their second child was born – another little girl whom they named Christine. But if Gustave was hoping for a reversal of the state of their marriage he was disappointed, as the relationship disintegrated even further.

Married life was not how Gustave imagined it to be – his wife complained bitterly about her constant tiredness and her unwillingness to look after their daughters, so Gustave took matters into his own hands, and sent Christine to live with his elder sister Isabelle, who also lived in Marigné.

In August 1910 Gustave and Clémence settled in Le Mans with their daughter Emilia, and on September 15th, 1911 Clémence gave birth again, to a third daughter whom they named Léa.[1]

Christine

Christine was happy at her Aunt Isabelle's. Isabelle had a deep mistrust of men but had always wanted to be a mother, so when she was given the opportunity to take in a baby to raise as her own, she jumped at the chance. Isabelle's own mother had been destroyed, at least in Isabelle's eyes, by numerous pregnancies, and she was adamant she was not going to go the same way. She had worked as a maid and when her elderly employer died, Isabelle was left a small inheritance. She was fiercely independent and greatly disapproved of Christine's mother for her various involvements with men. According to Isabelle, as long as a woman stayed away from men she would be safe.

But Christine absorbed her Aunt's hatred of men, and in turn developed her own distrust of them.

Rape

Sometime around Léa's birth, a shocking secret emerged. Clémence found out that her husband, Gustave, had raped their first born daughter, Emilia, who would have been only around ten at the time. Clémence reacted with fury, but she not only directed that fury at her husband but also at her daughter Emilia, whom Clémence believed had seduced Gustave. There was talk of Emilia not being Gustave's daughter, and Clémence assumed that the little girl had been a willing sexual partner to her father, and had enjoyed it.

Clémence took her revenge on both of them.

She divorced Gustave, as one would expect for such a heinous crime, but she also took revenge on Emilia, sending her away to a religious orphanage called Le Bon Pasteur. The orphanage had a reputation for harshness, and Clémence thought it might force her 'errant' daughter to mend her ways. At the same time, Clémence removed Christine from Isabelle's care and placed her alongside her sister at the orphanage. Baby Léa was given to a great-uncle to be looked after, and Clémence, now both husband and child free, obtained work as a maid.[2]

Léa

Léa stayed with her uncle until 1918, when she was around seven. When her uncle died, Clémence placed Léa into a religious institution in Le Mans[3], where she would stay until 1924.

Emilia

Not a lot is known about Emilia Papin, except that, after her time at Le Bon Pasteur, she decided to enter the convent and dedicate her life to the church. As far as records show, she spent the rest of her life there.[4]

Back to Christine

Christine was set to follow in her older sister's footsteps – she, too, wanted to join a convent. While she had had Emilia at Le Bon Pasteur with her, she had felt protected and loved, but with Emilia now in a convent, Christine found herself alone. The love she had felt for Emilia now had nowhere to go, as entering the convent no doubt meant excommunicating herself from her family. So Christine turned her affections towards her little sister, Léa.

Christine's plans were scuppered by Clémence, however. The woman had been furious when Emilia had joined the convent, as she had been getting to an age when she could go out to work and earn money to send to her mother. So when Christine decided she wanted the same life, Clémence put her foot down, exercising her parental rights.[5]

At that time, in France, the age of majority was 21, meaning that parents had the deciding say on what their children did up until that time. So Clémence, seeing her meal ticket disappearing the same way it had with Emilia, prevented Christine from joining a convent and instead committed her to a life of service.

Christine was well suited to the life of a maid – she had spent eight years at Le Bon Pasteur where she had been expertly taught in skills such as housekeeping and sewing.

Christine found work easily enough, but she was forced to leave several jobs because, according to her mother, the pay wasn't enough for her (Clémence's) needs.

When Léa was old enough, she too went into service, and the two sisters often worked together in the various homes of their employers.

The Lancelins

In 1926, when Christine was 22, she managed to secure a position with the Lancelin family in Le Mans.

René Lancelin was a retired lawyer, who lived at No. 6 rue Bruyère, with his wife, Léonie, and their grown-up daughter, Geneviève. The couple had another daughter who lived away from home.

When Christine had been working for the Lancelins for two months, she asked them if they would consider hiring Léa as well. Madame Lancelin was impressed with the standard of Christine's work, so she agreed to take on her younger sister too.

Life went on, with Christine working as the cook and Léa as the chambermaid. The girls were diligent with their work, putting in 12-14 hour days and working six and a half days a week. Their only time off was a half day on Sundays when the girls would attend church, dressed appropriately, with gloves and hats.

The sisters had no interests outside of each other and the church, apart from an occasional visit to a local medium, and the remainder of their time was spent in the attic room they shared. They showed no interest in meeting suitors, or dancing, or going to the movies.[6]

At first, it would seem that the sisters had a reasonable relationship with Madame Lancelin. When their employer found out that they were sending their wages to their mother, Clémence, she urged them to stop passing it on and keep it for themselves. She even went so far as to tell Clémence herself that her 'gravy train' had now stopped. The girls' wages were around 3000 francs per year, which amounts to around $2236 today.[7]

Because of Madame Lancelin's kindness, the sisters began referring to her as 'Maman' in private.

Although their living arrangements were basic – the sisters shared one small bed in the attic for instance – they had a balcony from which they could watch the people of Le Mans pass by. It was a relative luxury among the serving community.[8] Indeed, as servants go, the sisters had it better than most. There was always plenty to eat, and the girls had a heated bedroom, a luxury which many other servants of the time were denied.

The Tide Turns

After a few years, things began to take a downward turn in the Lancelin household. Although both the girls had an enviable reputation with regards to their work, their personalities seemed to cause some consternation among other people. Local shopkeepers found the girls to be aloof and reserved, and one woman, who herself had employed Christine for a couple of weeks, described her time with Christine as difficult, stating that she found the girl so touchy and rebellious that she was loath to ask her to do anything. Nonetheless, their professional standing was second to none – unlike other maids of the time, the sisters did not engage in any flirtations with local boys and applied themselves meticulously to their duties.

Despite Madame Lancelin's initial kindness in ensuring the girls got to keep their wages, she became an increasingly hard taskmaster and took to wearing white gloves to check that the sisters had left no dust anywhere.

Communication became stinted. Madame Lancelin would only communicate with Christine and not Léa, and even then it would invariably be via a typed message regarding their work rather than through actual conversation.

Monsieur Lancelin himself later admitted that he had never once spoken to Christine or Léa during their seven years of service in his house.[9]

Sisterly Love

The fact that the sisters spent so much time together alone in their room did not go unnoticed. Christine was also fiercely protective of Léa, and was apparently extremely jealous of Genevieve Lancelin, whenever she attempted to initiate conversation with the younger sister. On one of the girls' visits to the local medium, they had apparently been told that Christine had been Léa's husband in a past life, a belief which she seemed to act out. In fact, such was the abnormality of the closeness and affection the sisters shared for each other that Madame Lancelin and her family began to suspect that the two young women were engaged in sexual relations.[10]

The sisters were unnaturally close, described by some that knew them as obsessive. They would braid each other's hair, make clothes for each other, and spent every moment together, completely shunning any outside interests. On one occasion, Madame Lancelin took it upon herself to spy on the women and had her suspicions confirmed when she caught the sisters making love. One can only imagine the shock – at the time homosexuality was very much frowned upon, and when you add incest to the mix it became even more scandalous. To the girls, though, their behaviour probably felt completely normal. Their own father had raped their sister, and their Aunt had consistently warned against the perils of mixing with men.[11] Their father had disappeared from their lives after his sexual abuse of Emelia had come out, apparently fighting in World War One and subsequently re-marrying[12]) and they had found in each other the affection and love that their own mother had been unwilling or unable to provide. The love they had for each other was the only love they had ever truly known. Madame Lancelin decided to share what she had seen with the rest of her family, but for one reason or another no action was taken, and life carried on.

The situation became more strained after a particular incident involving Léa and Madame Lancelin. While cleaning the floor, Léa had missed a tiny scrap of paper, which Madame Lancelin noticed, and, enraged by the girl's inattention to detail, pinched Léa hard and viciously until she was forced to her knees to pick up the offending piece of paper. Léa, who was normally very quiet and withdrawn, told Christine *"She had better not try that again or I will defend myself."*[13]

Christine's Descent into Madness

Towards the end of 1932, Christine's behaviour began to change. She began to suffer explosive fits of anger which she directed at her younger sister, Léa. The previously loving, albeit unnatural, relationship became a frightening ordeal for the younger sister as she could do nothing but suffer her older sister's outbursts which came from nowhere. Her normally kind demeanour was slowly changing into that of someone totally alien to her.

The pair continued to perform their duties for the Lancelin family, but Christine was losing her grip on reality. She began to suffer from hallucinations – seeing and hearing things which were not there, and these episodes, which today would have been recognized as symptoms of paranoid schizophrenia, in turn, set off panic attacks in Léa, who could not cope with her sister's state of mind, and behaviour.

It was all about to come to a tragic and fatal head.

February 2nd, 1933

The late winter was making its presence felt in Le Mans on February 2nd, 1933. It was bitterly cold, and the wind was howling outside.[14] Madame Lancelin had spent the day shopping with her daughter, Genevieve, and the pair were due to meet Monsieur Lancelin at his brother in law's house for dinner later that evening. Christine and Léa were not expecting their employer home until late into the night.

One of Léa's jobs for that day had been to take a broken iron to the electrician's to be fixed. However, when she returned home and plugged it in ready to do some ironing, it shorted the power to the entire house. As the Lancelins weren't due home until late that night, Christine took the decision to leave fixing the fuse until the next morning.

However, Madame and Genevieve Lancelin did return home, sometime after 5.30 pm, and were annoyed to find the house in darkness. Christine met them at the door and explained that the iron had been fixed, but that when it had been plugged in it had shorted the power. Madame Lancelin was furious at this news and a row broke out.

It was enough to tip Christine over the edge.

The older sister grabbed a pewter jug and brought it down onto Madame Lancelin's head. Her daughter, Genevieve, heard the commotion and came rushing to her mother's aid, only to receive a similar blow. As Christine began to fight with Genevieve, Léa joined in, struggling with Madame Lancelin, who had managed to recover somewhat from the blow. As the fight continued in the darkness, Christine shouted: *"I'm going to massacre them."*

As the fight became more frenzied, Christine began to shout orders to her sister.

"Smash her head into the ground" and *"tear her eyes out"*!

Léa had always followed her older sister's orders, and she wasn't about to stop now. With her bare hands, she gouged Madame Lancelin's eyes out, while Christine did the same thing to Genevieve.

As the two women lay writhing, blind and in agony on the floor, the sisters went on the search for weapons with which to continue their brutal attack. Finding a knife and a hammer, they returned to the grisly scene, and systematically beat their employers with first the pewter jug, and then the hammer. Mercifully for the Lancelin women, death came at last. But, even though they could no longer feel it, their mutilation was far from over.

The Papin sisters then 'prepared' the bodies of the two women as if they were preparing a joint of meat for dinner, carving deep gashes into their flesh. Lifting the skirts of the two women over their heads, leaving them with no dignity whatsoever, the maids sliced into their thighs and buttocks. Their final act of humiliation was to smear Madame Lancelin's body with Genevieve's menstrual blood, basting her as they would baste a joint of beef.

The Discovery

While his wife and daughter were being slaughtered in their own home, Monsieur Lancelin was at first irritated, and then worried, when they failed to show up for dinner. He made the journey home to pick them up, but when he arrived he couldn't get in. The house was locked and bolted from the inside. He thought it strange that the maids hadn't answered the door, but decided that perhaps they hadn't heard him and that his wife and daughter had already left for Madame Lancelin's brother's house.

When he returned to his brother in law's house, however, there was still no sign of his wife or daughter, and Monsieur Lancelin began to worry. Enlisting the help of a dinner guest, he returned once more to his house, but he still could not get inside. Furthermore, the house was in darkness apart from a candle flickering in the window of the maids' attic bedroom.

Finally, he went to the police with his concerns.

One of the policemen who returned to the house with Monsieur Lancelin climbed the wall at the back of the house and gained entry through the kitchen door.

As he cautiously made his way through the house, his path lit only by his flashlight, the policeman could see no signs of a struggle. Everything was in place, giving no clues as to what had happened.

But as he climbed the stairs to the second floor, the beam of light fell on an object on the floor. Small, and round. At first, the policeman couldn't tell what it was, but as he looked closer, he realized to his horror that it was an eyeball.

It became clear to the policeman that more horrors were to come, and he called down to Monsieur Lancelin not to come any further into the house.

As he continued to climb the stairs, the officer stumbled upon the bodies of Madame and Genevieve Lancelin. Or rather, he assumed it was them, as their faces had been smashed with such ferocity that they were unrecognizable. Both women had had their eyes removed, and Madame Lancelin's eyeballs were discovered in the folds of the scarf she was wearing.

The officers were aware that in addition to the Lancelins, there were two maids living in the house. Assuming the bodies they had just discovered had been slaughtered by a madman, they climbed the second flight of stairs to the attic, fearing that they would also find the mutilated bodies of Christine and Léa. They were also mindful of the fact that the murderer, or murderers, might still be in the house.

The door to the maids' room was locked from the inside, and the gendarme could see candlelight flickering from within. Calls to the girls to open the door were futile, so the officers broke down the door, and entered the small attic room.

Christine and Léa Papin were huddled up in bed together, having carefully removed their blood stained clothes and washed their bodies, before putting on clean bedclothes and climbing into bed together.

Next to the bed was a blood soaked hammer.[15]

What Happened Next

The sisters were taken for questioning. Christine was unapologetic in her admission of guilt, explaining matter-of-factly what had happened when the Lancelin women had returned home. Describing the moment that Madame Lancelin lost her temper over the iron, Christine continued:

"Then I rushed down to the kitchen and went to fetch a hammer and a knife, and with both instruments my sister and I fought on our two mistresses, we stabbed [their] heads with a knife, Struck with a pot of tin which was placed on a small table on the landing. We changed the instruments several times from one to the other, that is to say, that I passed to my sister the Hammer to strike and she passed the knife to us, we did the same with the tin pot, and the victims screamed, but I do not remember that they spoke a few words. I went to lock the door and closed the door of the vestibule as well. I closed these doors because I liked it better than the police who noticed our crime before our boss. Then my sister and I went to wash our hands...because we had them full of blood, then we got into our room, we took off our belongings which were stained with blood, we put on a bathrobe, we closed the door to our room, and we went to bed Both in the same bed. This is where you found us when you broke the door. I do not have any regrets or, in other words, I cannot tell you if I do not have any, I prefer to have the skin of my bosses rather than that they have mine or that of my sister. I did not premeditate my crime, I had no hatred towards them, but I do not accept the gesture that Madame Lancelin had for me this evening."

Léa refused to give any account of the evening's events, only to say that she agreed with everything Christine had said, adding:

"Everything [my] sister told you is accurate, the crimes happened exactly as she told you. My role in this case is absolutely the one she told you. I struck as much as she did, and I assert that we had not premeditated to kill our patrons, the idea came to us instantly when we heard that

Madame Lancelin reproached us. [Like] my sister I have no regret for the criminal act we have committed...like my sister, I prefer to have the skin of my bosses rather than those who have had our own."[16]

The Trial

The Papin sisters were brought to trial in September 1933. It was an event which was followed by people all over France, and police had to be drafted in to help control the crowds.

In the run-up to the trial, Christine's behavior became more and more disturbing. The sisters had been separated after their arrest, and Christine displayed sexually driven behavior, calling out for her sister and writhing around on the floor in a sexual manner. She also began to experience the same hallucinations she had while she was with the Lancelins, and on one occasion attempted to gouge her own eyes out, resulting in her being restrained in a straight jacket.

Following this incident, Christine recanted her statement, claiming responsibility for both murders, and saying that Léa had had nothing to do with either of them. Léa, however, continued to take responsibility for her part, and Christine's attempts to free her sister were dismissed at the trial.

The sisters were both found guilty of murder. Christine was sentenced to death by guillotine, while Léa, who had only been charged with the murder of Madame Lancelin, received a lighter sentence of ten years' hard labor, as the jury believed that she had been heavily influenced by her older sister.

Christine's sentence was later commuted to life imprisonment, but she did not fare well. Pining for her beloved Léa, Christine became deeply depressed and stopped eating. She was transferred to an asylum in Rennes, but her condition never improved and she died in 1937 of *cachexia* – literally wasting away.

Léa, on the other hand, fared much better. She kept her head down and did what was asked of her, and after eight years she was released on good behavior. Extraordinarily, she settled in Nantes with her mother,

Clémence, where she assumed the name of Marie and gained employment as a chambermaid.[17]

Léa

In September 1966, an article ran in the newspaper *France-Soir*. A journalist had tracked Léa down and interviewed her. Although the article was factually incorrect, and somewhat moralizing, it gave readers a glimpse into the madness that had taken hold of the youngest Papin sister.

"I do what I can to keep my room simple so that my sister, who watches me from above (because I'm certain she is in Paradise), doesn't laugh at me. I pray for her. I pray for our mother who lived with me until she died. To help me, she said...and all at once I didn't pray anymore. Christine watches me. She is always beautiful and young. She smiles as in the old days: with irony! I come apart, I shrivel up, I sweat from fear, I faint...And there's a trunk in my room."

She talked about her work at the hotel, and the fear she felt every time she made a mistake - of the young chambermaids who worked with her, and the teasing they bestowed upon her.

But her last words to the journalist showed her lack of grasp on reality and the sad delusion she had created for herself.

"When I don't have to work anymore, I want to become Sister Marie, at Bon Pasteur, in Le Mans. I've been saving for it. At Bon Pasteur, one of my older sisters is a nun. I'll go back to her..."[18]

HUSBAND KILLER SHARI TOBYNE

ANA BENSON

When it comes to female killers, the most common type of crime is mariticide or murdering their husbands. There are many motivations behind taking someone's life but killing a person so close to you is often fueled by passion, financial gain, jealousy, or betrayal. The case of Shari Tobyne is the perfect example of a woman scorned. Her husband of thirty-five years wanted to divorce her due to the financial problems she caused by mishandling the couple's finances.

So one day before he was set to leave their rented house and move on, Shari snapped. She simply couldn't allow him to leave after so many years they spend together. Shari continued to live her life normally, but Arizona police started uncovering body parts from counties surrounding the city of Phoenix and they couldn't determine the exact identity of the deceased man. Worried Tobyne children alerted the law enforcement that their father was missing and this is where the story started to unravel.

It will soon be discovered that a loving mother and a grandmother murdered her husband in cold blood because leaving him was simply not an option.

Early life

Shari Tobyne was born on 24th of July, 1956 in Clifton, Kansas. She grew up in a rural area just outside of the city. Her parents owned a farm and her father was quite successful in his line of business. She was a happy, carefree girl who enjoyed spending time in nature and would often help her family by jumping in and completing difficult farm related tasks.

This is where she met her future husband, Dwight Tobyne. He lived just across the street from Shari and his parents ran their own agricultural business. Dwight loved Shari's personality and energy so he soon realized that he had a crush on her. However, he didn't want to make a move too quickly so he waited until he got a college acceptance letter to ask Shari to be his girlfriend. She was still in high school at that time.

Both Shari and Dwight wanted to achieve business success and escape their small town. They soon realized that they were a match made in heaven because they cheered each other on and offered great support when needed. The couple married in 1975 and they made a decision to move to Salina, Kansas to start their life as a husband and wife. They wanted to make a better future for their family and relocating to a big city was their best option.

Shari was a bit apprehensive at first but the fact that she had Dwight right there beside her made the transition a lot easier. Dwight started a semester at the University of Kansas, studying Animal Sciences while Shari wanted to be a perfect wife and keep their home in pristine conditions. The pressure was on Dwight and he simply had to succeed with his academic work because he was supposed to carry the Tobyne family to the business success eventually.

The couple's first child, Jennifer was born in 1977. They welcomed a baby boy, Brad only three years later. The family was growing but Dwight was still in college, trying to graduate. Shari was very stressed about the financial situation and they struggled to take care of their children. Dwight did his best to earn some extra money so he landed a part-time job in hopes it would cover the expenses.

Trading stocks and interests were all the rage back in the 1980s and Dwight though it would be a perfect opportunity to invest the money he had on his account and try his luck. It wasn't his field of study and he soon got lost in all the numbers and investment opportunities. He pretty much gambled away all of their family savings and they ended up getting evicted from their townhouse. They packed their things and moved back to their parents.

With a third child on its way, the Tobyne family was under a lot of stress. Dwight even though about leaving Shari because he felt like he had failed both her and their children. Being the provider was already very hard for him and the fact that he managed to spend all of their money created additional pressure. Moving back to their parents was another blow. The situation was dismal and both of them knew that they have to make some difficult decisions in near future.

The move and success

The Tobyne family wanted to have a new beginning so they packed their things and moved to Denver, Colorado. Dwight was ecstatic because he can continue his education up there and earn a master's degree that will certainly come in handy when it comes to finding employment in near future. He also landed a full-time job at a bank and the pay was quite good.

Inspired by the economic boom of the 1990s, Dwight Tobyne enrolled into a business school and earned a diploma after a couple of years. Combining everything he learned with smart ideas and investments, Dwight created a leasing company. It was exactly what Denver needed at the time and he knew it would be a success.

It took Dwight a few years to make some serious money and now the family was living comfortably in a large house. They had everything imaginable and Shari finally started to feel confident. She knew that Dwight was a hard worker but she did have doubts when the company was first started because she knew how it felt to lose money.

The Tobynes looked like a perfect family because they were wealthy, active in the community, and their children were successful in school. Shari loved the attention and enjoyed a classy lifestyle that was a complete opposite of the things they went through in Kansas. She felt the need to contribute to the wealth of her family so she got her real estate license. It was time to stop being a housewife and start doing things on her own.

Dwight supported his wife's decision to create her own business and they cheered each other on as usual. They would often collaborate and help each other out with work-related tasks. Everything seemed to go really well for the Tobynes and they continued to live large with their ever-growing wealth.

The first sign of trouble

In 2003, Shari and Dwight lived alone in their family house. The children have moved out and the two of them still ran their business successfully. One day, Shari told Dwight that she made some mistakes regarding one of her accounts and that the numbers were not adding up. Her client lost their money due to this mistake and Shari's real estate license was taken away. Her job and the real estate career were in jeopardy.

It was clear that Shari tried to commit some type of fraud but she was never prosecuted for that. The Tobynes had plenty of money left in the bank and since they were experts at the new beginnings, they thought it would be the perfect time to move somewhere warmer. Dwight told his friends that they were going to Arizona because the real estate opportunities down there are amazing. But the truth was they were fleeing the city because the majority of their neighbors were aware of Shari's bad business decisions and they needed to surround themselves with people who don't know them well.

They bought a huge house in Gilbert, Arizona which was as posh and classy as their previous residence. It was a part of a gated community outside of Phoenix and they felt right at home. Dwight continued with his leasing business and it seemed like Phoenix was really a good relocation choice because he was getting a lot of work there. Since Shari was not employed, she became very involved with the way Dwight ran his business. She started helping him out because she had plenty of free time on her hands. Shari was in charge of family finances.

But in 2008, Dwight started getting phone calls from his friends and clients who were asking about his health. The majority of them though that he was in a hospital. Dwight figured out that Shari was behind this and that she was telling them that he had a heart-attack. He got really worried and started going through his company's financial records. He noticed something alarming – he was missing a large amount of money and since Shari was in charge of the accounts, he asked her about it.

The confrontation was quite explosive, mostly because Dwight couldn't believe that she could do something like that to him. After all, they have been married for decades and stealing from his own company was simply shocking. Shari had an explanation for everything and she told Dwight that she took the money to pay the bills and other necessities. Dwight was still unconvinced and furious. He knew what she had done in Denver and this looked almost the same.

Just a couple of weeks after the fight, Shari contacted her children and she sounded distracted. They weren't sure what was happening but it was clear that something was very wrong. Dwight was at the house when he realized that he hadn't seen his wife for hours. After combing every room of their home, he went out to his neighbor's house and he found Shari laying on a couch. There was an empty pill bottle right beside her. Shari wasn't responding and he called an ambulance.

Once she was conscious, Shari explained that she did try to kill herself because she simply couldn't take it any longer. She hid important information from Dwight and he found everything out in the hospital. They were in serious debt and their accounts were pretty much emptied out. The reality came crashing down on Dwight and he couldn't hide the sadness from his face. His business was ruined and he worked hard for nothing. He was still in disbelief that his own wife could have done this.

The Tobynes had to sell their lavish house in the gated community in order to cover at least a portion of the debt. It was a psychological shock to both of them because they had to find a smaller place to live in. They were back at the square one. So they gathered their things and moved to Scottsdale, Arizona.

The tensions between the pair were high and Dwight was on the fence about divorcing Shari. He made a decision to leave her in autumn of 2009 because he couldn't forget the things she put him through.

However, they did their best to appear as normal as possible in front of their children. But when Dwight failed to show up at the Thanksgiving dinner in November of 2009, Shari confessed that Dwight left her and moved to Mexico. None of their children could have predicted that Shari was not telling the truth about the divorce and that the reality was more sinister.

The murder of Dwight Tobyne

In November of 2009, Shari bought herself a gun. She started practicing shooting at a local gun range and her last visit to that place was on 22nd of November. It looked like the divorce was the final straw that made her think about murdering her own husband. After getting a sense of how the gun worked, all she needed to do is find the right time to shoot Dwight. The exact date of the murder is still unknown but sometime between 24th and 28th of November 2009, Shari entered the couple's bedroom and fired the gun at Dwight Tobyne. It is presumed that she shot him in the head.

She then wrapped his lifeless body into the carpet that was already soaking up the blood and dragged him to a garage where she proceeded to chop his corpse into pieces. She took her time with each and every part, first cutting off the arms and feet. She did use a saw, as well as some other tools, but Shari also tore away some pieces herself. The garage was a mess and she needed to get rid of every single evidence that could connect her to the murder.

After wrapping the parts into cellophane and carpet cutouts, she loaded them up in her car and started making rounds through adjacent counties, dropping them in remote areas by an interstate. She did her best to leave them a bit away from the road in hopes that the animals would drag the parts even further into the wilderness. She was certain that this was the way to keep the police off her trail and ensure that she will not get caught. She then cleaned the crime scene with plenty of bleach, removing each and every spec of blood from the floor and walls. She presumably got rid of the saw and other tools as well.

She kept Dwight's cell phone and intended to pretend like he simply left her. She planned to contact her children every now and then via text messages and e-mails so they would think that Dwight was alive and well, soaking up the sun in Mexico. Since Shari wouldn't make any profit from her husband's death, the only explanation was that this was a crime of passion. They were married for almost thirty-five years and Dwight simply couldn't leave her right then after everything they went through. Shari's emotions obviously get the best of her and the result was gruesome.

The discovery of the crime

Even though Dwight missed the Thanksgiving dinner, the biggest red flag was the fact that he wasn't present at the birth of the Tobyne's second grandchild. He did contact his children via text messages so they though he was alive and well. But when he didn't show up at the hospital, his oldest daughter alerted the police. It was July of 2010 and the law enforcement immediately started working on this case.

The Tobyne children told the authorities that their father wanted to move to Oklahoma but their mother told them that he went to Mexico. The investigators were certain that the story was false so they focused their attention on Shari since she was the last known person to see him alive. She was living with her children at the time because she had to move out from the condo she shared with her husband and didn't have enough money to support herself on her own. When they brought Shari for the first interview, she denied everything. Shari told them that she had no idea where her husband was at the moment and that he hadn't contacted her in months.

She was released but the police investigators did sense that something was very wrong with her statements. They decided to put her under surveillance in order to see what she would do next and monitor any possible suspicious activities. Just like it was expected, Shari started acting oddly. The police officers saw her disposing of something in a dumpster and when they got there, they discovered a couple of clothing items, as well as pieces of a gun. She then proceeded to clean the trunk of her car which was even more alarming to the detectives because it looked like she was getting rid of the possible evidence.

Then they managed to locate Dwight's Ford pickup truck at a parking lot. It was obvious that the car was there for months but no one had reported it because it was parked in front of a residential building and there were a lot of vehicles there on a daily basis. There was no physical evidence of the crime anywhere in the car which meant that Shari probably didn't use it for body disposal. Checking the cell phone records was the next step and the investigators discovered that both of their phones were at the same location during the time frame when the possible murder occurred, as well as afterward. So Shari's story about Dwight leaving for Mexico in November of 2009 was clearly false because he wouldn't leave his phone behind. It was time to bring her back to the station for a second interview.

Shari broke down under pressure and told the detectives a whole new story. She said that she bought the gun with an intention to use in for her own suicide. Shari was feeling horrible after everything she had done with her husband's money and she wanted to end her life. The fact that Dwight was leaving her added to her depression and she simply couldn't continue to live anymore.

She brought the gun to their bedroom wanting to shoot herself in the head. Instead, Dwight who was there as well noticed the gun, grabbed it from her hands and unintentionally pulled the trigger while they were fighting for the weapon. He shot himself and was losing a lot of blood quickly. He was soon dead. Shari then said that she was lost and scared, knowing that no one would believe her story. So she quickly wrapped her husband in the sheets and dragged him to her car. She drove off to a remote location and left his body there.

Shari insisted that the death was an accident and that she didn't mean to hurt her husband. She volunteered to take the investigators to the place where she dumped the body. Listening to her directions, they went east of Scottsdale and started combing through the area. They couldn't find any traces of Dwight's corpse even though they covered a wide field around the alleged dump site. They knew that a lot of time has passed since the killing and that animals could have dragged the body someplace else, but they couldn't find anything that could indicate that a corpse was there in the first place.

The investigators placed Shari in the jail and continued to question other possible witnesses that could shed some light on this case. It was obvious that Shari's story was either incomplete or entirely false. They approached the owner of the apartment which Tobyne's were renting at the time of the murder. She told the police that the carpet in the master bedroom was brand new after Shari left the condo and that she also noticed a strong smell of bleach in the garage. It was a minor clue at the time because the investigators knew that Shari was an obsessive cleaner and she would often go around the house with pure bleach in order to disinfect all the surfaces. However, once they put the pieces back together, the bleach will play an important part in the investigation because it was used to clean up the scene.

Finding Dwight Tobyne

Back in December of 2009, prior to the missing person report which was filed by Dwight's children, dismembered body parts were found near a highway in Pinal County, namely legs without feet. The cuts were partially clean but they could see that the murderer did apply some force and they were more focused on tearing off the limbs than on keeping everything pristine. The police officers were sure that a saw of some kind was used in the process. The parts were collected by the police and sent for further analysis. The second set of body parts was discovered in La Paz County only a couple of days later. Hikers bumped onto a man's torso near the main road and alerted the authorities who once again collected the evidence.

Two police departments got into contact and they examined their findings in order to determine that the parts belonged to the same person. And then, three days later, a person traveling on a motorbike noticed something strange on the side of the road near Sugarloaf exit. The authorities in the area were already aware that they had a dismembered body on their hands and the remains were transported to Pinal County to make sure they also came from the same victim. The results were positive but the identity of the man was still unknown because they hadn't found the hands so fingerprint search was out of the question. As a matter of fact, some remains are still missing to this day.

The investigators who were working on Dwight Tobyne's case were aware of the mystery man who was found in three counties and they took a DNA swab from his parents in order to see if it was the match. The dates of the discoveries overlapped their murder theory and the detectives feared the worst. But before they delivered it to the medical examiner's office, they compared Dwight's physical description with the collected body parts. Hugh Lockerby, a detective from Scottsdale who worked on this case said: "A left leg was recovered first. A couple of days later, north of Phoenix, right leg was discovered. One hundred miles west of Phoenix a complete torso was uncovered. I asked could they give me a little description of the race, the height, the weight, and I am listening as they are telling me this and that is the exact description of Dwight Tobyne."

When the tests came back positive, they confirmed that it was, in fact, Dwight Tobyne. Since Shari Tobyne didn't mention any dismemberment of the body in her second statement, they had enough evidence to prove that she was lying. It was time to confront her and try to find out what exactly happened on that fatal night in November of 2009.

Shari pleaded not guilty in front of a judge and repeated her story about the accidental shooting. Her lawyer, Anne Phillips asked the judge to allow a psychological evaluation of her client because she was impossible to communicate with. She refused to provide her with any helpful details and Phillips thought that Shari might need some psychological help due to the fact that she was suicidal in the past.

Her attorney also wanted to be sure that Shari Tobyne did understand the charges properly. It looked like she was not fully there and her responses were sparse, providing Phillips with short answers only. The judge allowed a psychiatric examination and it was confirmed that Shari was responsive and aware of her actions. She didn't suffer from psychosis or depression. There were no underlying psychological issues and she was capable of attending her own trial.

However, the way she acted after the murder told the psychiatrist who conducted the evaluation that Shari Tobyne was a textbook sociopath. Not every person has the ability to separate their emotions and continue acting normally after a crime like this. She was sticking to her story no matter how unlikely it sounded and it seemed like Shari did really believe in her version of the shooting.

The trial

As previously mentioned, Shari Tobyne pleaded not guilty in the initial hearing. The state had a solid case against her even though they had no witnesses to the murder itself. She did confess to accidental shooting so she clearly was involved to some degree. However, her actions after the gun went off told a different story about a very violent body dismemberment and disposal. The fact that Shari lied to the authorities about the location of the body dump added a whole new layer to the case. She obviously didn't want the body to be found and hoped that the animals would do the dirty work for her.

Shari was facing the charges of a first-degree murder, as well as a concealment of the body parts. Since she did have some sketchy history regarding the financial fraud, the authorities had enough evidence to add it to the charges as well. They were asking for the death penalty. Shari's attorney didn't have much to work with but she repeated her old story about the accidental shooting. The verdict could have gone in both ways at that point, depending on the jury. So instead of going on a trial, Shari decided to end it as quickly as possible.

Shari Tobyne pleaded guilty on May 19th, 2012, ending the trial. It was the only way she could avoid the death penalty. That was a clever decision because her claims were simply not strong enough to convince everyone that she didn't shoot her husband on purpose. So instead she received life in prison and an additional thirty-one years for the financial fraud.

The children were in shock from the beginning of this case and they had a difficult time accepting the fact that their loving mother could actually kill their father. Shari Tobyne remains behind the bars and it is unclear when and if she would get an opportunity for an appeal.

ADRIANA VASCO : KILLER FOR HIRE

68

JESSI GILLMAN

"Somebody just assassinated them."

When a security guard discovered a car parked along the shoulder of the Ortega Highway on November 20, 1999, with the engine running and the lights on, he assumed it was a couple of kids making out. Instead, he found the bullet-riddled bodies of a prominent Huntington Beach doctor and his optometrist wife sprawled across the vehicle's front seat.

"The car is running, the lights are on – he walks up to the car and looks through the driver's side window, and he gets a glimpse of a horrific scene," said Michael Fleeman, who wrote about the murder of Kenneth Stahl and Carolyn Oppy-Stahl in his book, *Deadly Mistress*.

Stahl, 57, and his wife had been out celebrating her 44th birthday the day before when he suddenly pulled over on the side of the road. The couple was about 30 miles from home – driving in the opposite direction. Just two hours later, investigators were digging for clues that would help them solve the murder – with no leads, no obvious motives, and no witnesses.

"When I arrived there, the driver had a gunshot wound near the bridge of his nose," said Jim McDonald, a senior investigator with the Orange County sheriff's department who worked on the case. "It appeared to be an entry wound – it looked like he'd been shot in the face. There was also another entry wound in the upper part of his chest."

McDonald said Stahl was still upright in the driver's seat, with his seatbelt still securely fastened. The passenger, Oppy, was laying down in the car, with her head near the centre console and at least one leg hanging out the open passenger door. McDonald added that she had multiple gunshot wounds to both the front and back of her body.

Investigators quickly ruled out the possibility that the scene was the result of a murder-suicide between the husband and wife, as no gun had been located in the car. There was also no evidence of a robbery, as both victims still had their wallets and plenty of cash when they were discovered.

"It was as if they'd pulled over and somebody just assassinated them," Fleeman said.

The case went unsolved for more than ten months before it was passed off to a new team, Detectives Brian Meaney and Felipe Villalobos. Veterans of the force with a solid, effective partnership, Meaney and Villalobos got to work immediately – reading over old case files, interviewing people, and bouncing around possible theories. Eventually, they made a breakthrough.

"It's a tale of intrigue, a tale of murder," said Orange County Sheriff Mike Carona. "But most importantly, it's a tale of some outstanding police work, some outstanding detective work."

While going through Stahl's cell phone log, the detectives saw the same number pop up with consistent frequency. The number belonged to a medical receptionist named Adriana Vasco, who worked at one of Stahl's clinics. When they interviewed the receptionist, a potential motive began to take shape. Vasco wasn't just the receptionist – she'd been having an affair with Stahl for many years, and he'd been providing her with regular financial support.

This wasn't the first time Stahl had cheated on a spouse. Already twice divorced, Oppy's sister Linda Dubay said Stahl had engaged in a series of affairs. Oppy had considered the possibility of seeking a divorce herself, saddened and angry with her husband's many infidelities, but according to Dubay, she maintained hope that Stahl would change.

"She had put up with so much and got used to it," said Dubay. "Somehow, the unknown is more scary than the known."

No matter how much effort Oppy put into the marriage, Dubay said she received little in return. According to Dubay, Stahl struggled to meet the expectations his family had for him – his father was a well-respected surgeon and CEO of a hospital, while Stahl worked as an anaesthesiologist.

"(Stahl) needed the ego boost of his affairs – usually with divorced nurses, single mothers, needy individuals," Dubay said.

Vasco was a perfect fit.

The black sheep

"She never really knew her father, didn't seem to get along well with her mother," said Fleeman, who heavily researched Vasco's background for his book, *Deadly Mistress*.

Born in Mexico as the product of a rape, Vasco suffered both physical and sexual abuse at the hands of her stepfather before leaving her family's home at the age of 16. The next few years, she "bounced around" the homes of friends and relatives, according to Detective Felipe Villalobos.

"She was like the black sheep of the family," said Deborah Burns, the manager at Vasco's Anaheim apartment. "She used to always say that."

However, Vasco quickly discovered that her looks and sex appeal could get her anything she wanted or needed – but she struggled to find a meaningful relationship. Her history of abuse had also given her "an almost pathologically bad taste in men," said Fleeman.

"She was very, very sexual," he explained. "Her exotic Latin looks attracted many men, and all of them said she was a sexual dynamo – they couldn't get enough of her. But she never had any kind of relationship that lasted very long."

At 25, one of Vasco's failed relationships left her a single mom – but in 1992, her luck started to change when she met Dr. Kenneth Stahl at her new job as a medical receptionist at a pain clinic.

"Stahl was a 57-year old anaesthesiologist that had set up a couple of his own businesses, pain clinics, "said Senior Prosecutor Dennis Conway. "At first, they were just friendly with each other, but then they started sharing details about their personal lives with one another."

Vasco and Stahl bonded over their struggles with intimate relationships. Stahl was excited that a much younger woman was paying him attention, while Vasco was flattered to have a well-established older man interested in more than just her body. After about a year, the pair finally gave in to the undeniable attraction that had formed between them.

"They developed a romantic relationship, and a very passionate sexual relationship," Fleeman said. "(Vasco) gave him, by all accounts, this wild and crazy sex life that he had never had before."

According to Fleeman, Vasco's behaviour with Stahl was consistent with her "pattern" – using sex to manipulate men into doing anything she wanted. By fulfilling his sexual fantasies, it appeared Vasco had Stahl wrapped around her finger.

"Friends of hers that she worked with said she would go to lunch with him and then come back and have five or seven hundred dollars with her," said Conway. "He bought her a couple of cars – and helped her out pretty regularly for about five or six years."

Stahl's bank records indicated a withdrawal of $20,000 in cash from his checking account – an unusual transaction, considering his account history. According to his estate executor, that money was never located or associated with a corresponding expense. During the same time period, Vasco came to work wearing several pieces of brand-new jewellery.

Vasco even depended on Stahl to cover her living expenses, according to the manager of her Anaheim condominium building.

"She said, 'you don't have to worry about rent, he'll pay for my rent,'" said Burns. "I saw him, off and on, come to the apartment building. He tried to always sneak in and sneak out, because he didn't want people to see him. But then, later on in the relationship, I would see him at the pool with her and the kid."

Still, Vasco initially denied the affair when police questioned her about her relationship with Stahl. She claimed that she'd only spoken to him on the morning before he was killed to discuss problems she was having with a computer and printer he was helping her repair. She added that Stahl had mentioned taking Oppy out for her birthday, but insisted he hadn't told her where they would be going.

Only three months later, Vasco admitted to the affair. This time, she told police that her relationship with Stahl ended in 1996, when she claimed he refused to leave his wife. In another interview, in October 2000, Vasco said that after she ended the affair with Stahl, she began seeing another man named Greg Stewart.

Vasco and Stewart had met at a mental hospital. The relationship between the two has been described as "tumultuous," plagued with drug use and violence. During this relationship, court documents allege that Vasco and Stahl remained close, and she said he "was always going to be there" for her.

However, officers began to doubt Vasco's story after speaking with her supervisor, Susana Torres-Bivian. According to Torres-Bivian, Vasco claimed to still be "dating" Stahl in 1999 – detailing the "long-term relationship" they had and giving Torres-Bivian the impression that this affair was ongoing. Vasco had also asked Torres-Bivian not to tell the police about her relationship with Stahl.

Torres-Bivian added that in the late summer of 1999, Vasco told her she'd started dating "Tony," a maintenance worker in Vasco's apartment building. It didn't conflict with her relationship with Stahl, Torres-Bivian said Vasco claimed – the men knew each other and were fine with the arrangement.

"Can you make her disappear?"

Vasco met Tony Satton when he used his maintenance man's passkey to let himself into Vasco's Anaheim apartment to repair her sink. When she told him not to barge into her home, "he responded by going into her bedroom," said Fleeman in his book, *Deadly Mistress*.

"Well, it began that way, (and) every day after that he started coming," Vasco recalled.

The relationship began innocently enough, with "civil" conversations whenever Satton dropped by. But eventually, he asked Vasco if she knew where he could buy marijuana. Since she'd started attending church and was living a sober life, Vasco told him she didn't – but she finally relented and sought out a dealer for Satton.

"That's how he started," she said. "And then he wanted some speed, so I got that for him, too… Before you know it, I started using again."

Vasco and Satton would get high together, and he would open up about his life back in North Carolina – past violence, encounters with police. He told her she needed to keep her mouth shut about his criminal history, even threatening to hurt Vasco's daughter, Ashley.

"He goes, 'I personally won't do it, but I'll have somebody come and get her and you'll never see her,'" said Vasco.

By this time, Stahl was getting desperate. His health was failing, and he wanted out of his stale marriage. Despite his healthy diet and daily exercise regimen, Stahl struggled with heart problems. At only 37 years old, Stahl underwent a triple-bypass surgery, followed by numerous angioplasty treatments. In July 1999, he pulled through a quadruple-bypass that doctors had given him only a 20 per cent chance of surviving.

"Stahl was going to die very soon," Villalobos said. "He wanted things to happen quickly."

Although legal records revealed that Stahl and Oppy had signed a prenuptial agreement, Stahl had told Vasco that he was afraid a divorce would "ruin him." He also admitted that his mother was very fond of Oppy, and she would be significantly hurt if he left his wife. That meant he needed to find another solution to free himself of his commitment to Oppy.

An electrician named Richard Anaya, who had previously been involved with a gang, told police that the doctor had made an "unusual late night proposal" after he'd been hired to do some electrical work about a year before the murders took place.

"He just said, 'I need somebody to take care of my wife, you know, she's making my life hell, and, you know, I was just wondering if you knew anybody,'" Anaya testified. "And I was like, 'wait a minute, man, are you joking around?'"

Anaya told the jury that he thought Stahl had been drinking, but that the look on Stahl's face was very serious. He led Stahl in a prayer and left – adding that he felt that Stahl's outlook had "improved."

In fact, Stahl was still determined to find a way out. Vasco recalled him saying, "that bitch, I can't stand her anymore. I want her gone. Can you make her disappear? Do you know anybody?"

At first, Vasco didn't. But as she learned more about Satton's violent past, it started to look as though there might be a solution to Stahl's problem. Satton claimed to have been part of an assassination group in North Carolina, and Vasco claimed she was drunk and on drugs when she told Satton about Stahl.

"He told me about people he had in Carolina that would take care of people," Vasco testified. "So I told him I have a doctor friend that wants to take care of his wife."

According to Vasco, she tried to back out of the arrangement by telling Satton that she was just kidding – but he refused to take no for an answer. She claimed he threatened to hurt her or her family if she didn't follow through, or if she told anyone about the deal. Eventually, Vasco said, Satton told her he needed money and demanded she get in touch with Stahl. Vasco complied.

"His demeanor, use of drugs, and paranoid behaviour alarmed her," said a court document, "and he routinely carried a shotgun at his side."

According to Detectives Villalobos and Meaney, the men allegedly came to an agreement – Stahl would pay Satton $30,000 to carry out the murder, then create a diversion and skip town.

Vasco told Stahl that Satton "was scary" and begged him to call off the plan. Instead, Stahl gave her an envelope full of cash and told her to deliver it to Satton. From then on, Vasco said, she didn't speak with either man about the arranged hit. In a statement to police, Vasco even claimed she was angry with Stahl for "putting her in the situation" which she felt was "wrong."

"I told (Stahl), 'please call it off,' and he wouldn't listen," she said. "I cried, 'please, please.' Nobody has any idea how bad I wanted to stop it."

In September, Vasco alleged, she successfully stalled a previous murder plot – and again attempted to persuade Stahl to back out of it again in November. This time, Stahl refused. According to Vasco's confession to police, Stahl pressured her by reminding her of everything he had done for her over their nine-year relationship.

"He just said, 'what about me? You want me to suffer all these years? You want to see me suffer the rest of my life?'" Vasco recalled, admitting that Stahl had been talking about killing his wife since as early as 1995.

However, Stahl was unaware that Vasco was having an affair with Satton – and Vasco didn't know that Satton was actually Dennis Earl Godley, a felon from Bellarthur, North Carolina, on the run from police in two states. She also didn't know about Godley's history of obsessive jealousy, when it came to his women.

Best laid plans

On November 19, Vasco had plans to visit with her daughter's grandmother, Nancy Stewart. The visit was cancelled, however, when Vasco told Nancy that she was feeling "stressed out" and needed some time to herself – to take a drive along the scenic Ortega Highway. According to an interview with the Orange County Register, she also met with Stahl and Godley to confirm the details of the planned hit.

According to Vasco's testimony, after meeting at the parking lot where Stahl and Godley first met, Stahl told her to drive up Ortega Highway while he followed close behind. When Godley told her to stop, he got out of the car and "took target practice at a sign." Vasco said she once again told Stahl about the threats Godley had made against her and her family, and begged him to reconsider.

The next day, Stahl called Vasco at work. Torres-Bivian said Vasco had left work early, so he said he would try her at home. According to Stahl's telephone records, he and Vasco spoke four or five times that day.

Vasco had plans that evening to attend a quinceanera with her neighbour, Belen Lopez. According to Lopez, Godley and Vasco stopped by the apartment to explain that they wouldn't be able to accompany her to the birthday party, claiming that they had "another commitment" to attend to. During this discussion, Lopez said, Godley was holding an empty shotgun case.

Godley and Vasco then went to a gas station on Ortega Highway, where they waited for the Stahls' car, a silver 1996 Dodge Stratus, to appear.

A big surprise

After celebrating Oppy's birthday at a restaurant in Mission Viejo, Stahl drove his wife east on Ortega Highway – a remote and winding road through the San Juan Capistrano foothills. They were headed away from their home, but Oppy didn't mind – she was glad to spend a romantic evening with her husband, whose history of infidelity had strained their marriage.

"She called that day and told us (Stahl) had a big surprise for her," said Linda Dubay, Oppy's sister. "She sounded hopeful."

The "big surprise" wouldn't be good for Oppy. Stahl pulled over onto the shoulder, leaving the engine running. Orange County sheriff's Captain Steve Carroll said that at this point, Stahl knew Vasco and Godley would show up to shoot his wife – "he's not expecting to get killed," Carroll added.

According to Vasco, she waited in the car while Godley approached the Stahls' car. She said she heard him ask if everything was okay, and then heard gunshots and Oppy's screams.

"She was saying, just, 'oh my god!' and yelling," Vasco said. "I didn't turn around. It was killing me."

Vasco claimed that she then contemplated leaving, but Godley returned to the car to reload his weapon – and pointed the gun at her. She said Godley asked her where she was going, and then said, "I was ready to pop you."

Godley then returned to Stahl's car, where Vasco heard him fire more gunshots. When he came back to the car, he told Vasco that he'd shot both Oppy and Stahl – to eliminate a potential witness. Detectives are still unsure if this is entirely true, or if Godley killed Stahl because he was jealous of the relationship between the doctor and Vasco.

"(Stahl) didn't see it coming," Villalobos said. "He thought he was taking care of her, and then – boom! – he got his."

According to Vasco, Godley had turned on Stahl because he hadn't followed the agreed-upon rules. During the hit, Godley had requested that Stahl keep his hands visible at all times by leaving them on the steering wheel – and when he didn't, Godley shot him.

Vasco gave Torres-Bivian a ride to work the Monday after the slayings, and according to Torres-Bivian, she appeared to be in shock as she told her about Stahl's death. Torres-Bivian said Vasco said "they" killed Stahl and his wife.

After committing the murders, Godley fled. Vasco told people that her relationship with "Tony" had ended after she'd caught him with another woman, but the two stayed in contact even after Godley returned to North Carolina.

The Weasel

Sergeant Ron Smith, with the Pitt County sheriff's department in Greenville, North Carolina, had been trying to arrest Godley for more than a year – ever since Godley had jumped through the window of his mobile home, kicked a deputy in the head, and disappeared into the surrounding woods.

"The Weasel – that's what we call him here, because he keeps escaping," Smith said. "In twenty years of service, he is one of the meanest men I have met. You look into his eyes, and they look black."

After Godley escaped, Smith asked informants across the county to tell him if the Weasel ever turned up again – and finally, in August 2000, Smith found him. The Weasel was finally brought in on robbery charges from nearly two years before, but it would be another two months before police would connect Godley to the murders in California.

An alert was sent from a department in Orange County, asking for help locating alleged murder suspect Tony Satton. The message was accompanied by a photograph of a man Smith had come to be very familiar with.

"Soon as I saw that picture, I knew it was the Weasel," Smith said.

Still, Godley denied his involvement with the murders during interviews with Meaney and Villalobos – but arrest warrants were issued for both Godley and Vasco on December 11.

"They are making it look like we (he and Vasco) were in this mad love affair and plotting and all these things," said Godley during a telephone interview from Tidewater Regional Jail in Suffolk, Virginia, where he awaited extradition following his arrest. "That's complete (baloney). I think it's a huge conspiracy and I'm the scapegoat."

Orange County police, however, were pleased to put the case behind them. According to Orange County Sheriff Michael Corona, "people who commit crimes like these need to know it may not be today, it may not be tomorrow – but someday, we are going to get them."

Learned helplessness

At her trial, Vasco testified that she didn't truly believe the murders would ever take place – and didn't intend the deaths of either victim. Her case was supported by a clinical psychologist, Dr. Nancy Kaser-Boyd, who specialized in family violence.

According to Kaser-Boyd, Vasco exhibited "common features" of both battered women's syndrome and post-traumatic stress disorder, including "learned helplessness" and denial. Kaser-Boyd claimed these stemmed from "repeated violent acts against her," including the abuse she suffered as a child as well as in a number of subsequent relationships.

Defense counsel used this to argue that Vasco "lacked the requisite intent" for a murder charge, and for the special circumstance allegations of lying in wait and multiple murder. The intimidation Vasco faced from Godley's persistent threats contributed to her "learned helplessness" and denial – demonstrating that she did not intend to help carry out the planned hit.

However, this defense was disputed by Deputy District Attorney Dennis Conway, who argued that Vasco was "not the type of woman where men can just march into your life and control you." He also informed the jury that Vasco had a past conviction of physically abusing a boyfriend.

The jury also heard from James Stewart, Vasco's daughter's paternal grandfather. In his testimony, he recalled going to a gun shop with Vasco in 1999. According to James, she'd pointed out a .357 Magnum revolver, claiming she'd bought the same kind of gun for her boyfriend, "Tony" – the same kind of gun that had been used to kill Stahl and Oppy.

"(Vasco) knew first-hand Godley was a dangerous, violent, paranoid sociopath," stated court documents. "The jury reasonably could conclude it was foreseeable such a violent individual would have an incentive to eliminate Stahl as a witness after Stahl paid him the entire amount under the murder contract."

A request was made by the defense to reduce Vasco's first-degree conviction for Oppy's murder, which would have made her eligible for parole after serving part of the sentences for each slaying. However,

Orange County Superior Court Judge Francisco P. Briseno denied the request.

According to a Los Angeles Times article published on November 26, 2002, Vasco "held her lawyer's hand and cried" as the jury read their verdict.

"She's a tough, street-smart person," said juror Donald Tobias, a retired chiropractor who lived in Placentia. "(The panel) felt that as long as she wasn't intoxicated or high, she had a pretty good idea this would happen."

Although Vasco's confession to police was thrown out by a judge who found that it had been "coerced," she was still convicted of first degree murder and was sentenced to life in prison with no possibility of parole. Godley pleaded guilty to murder, receiving the same sentence – however, he maintains that he only shot Stahl, claiming Oppy was murdered by Vasco.

"He recognized he committed this crime, and he's really remorseful for his part," said Godley's lawyer, Assistant Public Defender Denise Gragg.

KILLER BABE : THE TRUE STORY OF BRITTANY HOLBERG

82

Brittany Holberg was a twenty-three years old prostitute when she was convicted of murdering 80-year-old A.B. Towery Jr, stabbing him over sixty times.

The controversy surrounding the case centered around the relationship of Brittany and Towery prior to the killing. Brittany argued that Towery was a client who went into a rage when he found drugs on her person. He attacked her and she retaliated in self-defense.

Further investigation would reveal otherwise, however, as Brittany would use numerous household items in a brutal assault on the elderly man.

She fled the scene only to be caught at a McDonald's after police received a tip from a witness who saw her on "America's Most Wanted."

With her good looks and well-proportioned body, Brittany has remained in the spotlight as she was featured in a Maxim Magazine article as one of the "hottest women on death row".

Brittany still sits on death row today with her case being appealed on the numerous levels in the court system.

EARLY LIFE

Brittany was born on January 1, 1973, in Amarillo, Texas.

Accounts on Brittany's home life vary as she would manipulate according to the needs of her listener. To her probation officer, she informed them that her home life was "good" and that she "had everything that she ever wanted". She would often describe her mother as her best friend.

During other occasions, however, Brittany would paint a different story.

She would describe her parents as being "hippie-drugsters". Brittany would state that she was close to her mother but never knew her father, a heroin addict who was in and out of the Texas prison system. Her mother would later marry a man named John Schwartz with the couple marrying and divorcing four times.

They would drink heavily and openly smoke weed in front of the young Brittany who would be sexually assaulted by a babysitter at the age of five. When she was twelve, one of her aunts was murdered and according to Brittany "everything fell apart" at home. Her parents would leave her unattended as they indulged in pot and booze.

"They just stopped working," Brittany said. "They just let everything go."

She would be gang raped by two men who confronted her in an alley behind her home when she was thirteen.

Brittany would then spend the majority of her time living with her grandmother. By the age of sixteen, however, she would run away with her boyfriend Ward. The two would make it as far as California, get married, and have a young daughter named Mackenzie.

The union would not last long, however. Brittany would divorce Ward and move back to her native Amarillo. Ward would take Mackenzie and move to Tulsa, Oklahoma.

Brittany would state that she suffered a knee injury and would become addicted to pain medication during treatment. She would then graduate to harder drugs like cocaine.

In and out of rehab, Brittany's life spiraled out of control. She could manipulate with the best of them, however, and would escape from the Midland Halfway House with the help of a female counselor.

Brittany would hang out with the drug-using crowd and her own habits were out of control. To support her addiction, Brittany began working as a prostitute.

This would put her in harm's way on many an occasion as she would get gang-raped and beaten severely.

The assault would put her in the hospital but she would resume "tricking" when she was released.

"At that point in her life, Brittany was incorrigible," forensic psychologist Paula Orange said."Numerous people had reached to her and tried to help. She had extended family members trying to help. Friends trying to help. Even church outreach workers. All to no avail. The drugs had taken root and she was dead set on manipulating everyone around her. Family, roommates, church members, doctors, dentists, and pharmacists would all fall victim to her schemes to get drugs."

By 1993, Brittany was a full-blown drug-addicted prostitute with the rap sheet to prove it. In April of that year, she would steal a gun from her step-father. She then passed over $1300 in "hot" checks and applied for several store credit cards using a fake name.

Brittany and one of her aunts would run a scam on dentists, lying to them about their pain levels in order to get prescription medication. When the prescription drugs ran out, she would return to street drugs like cocaine and heroin. Arrests would follow and Brittany would be charged in Hale County with drug possession, paraphernalia, and public intoxication.

Upon her release, Brittany would proceed to steal her mother's car and forge checks in her name. The prostitution continued unabated as well as she stole the wallet from one of her "tricks" who pressed charges.

While in jail for the theft, Brittany would be introduced to Ella Gibbs and Patricia Karnes who ran the ministry in the Randall County Jail. The women tried to get Brittany on the right track and introduce her to Christianity.

"I wanted to reassure Brittany that she is a valuable person, that her life has great potential, and that this is the mortal portion of an eternal life," Karnes said. " Brittany is an eternal being and through the many prayers from my [prayer] group [in Lubbock,] I have been led to come back into this child's life to support her here, to encourage her, to find her courage from the Holy Spirit within her, and to let her know that there is a human being mortal person who will stand beside her and see the good in her and support whatever God plans for the rest of your [sic] life."

A.B. TOWERY

Towery was by all accounts a nice man. His son would bristle at the idea that he was Brittany's "sugar daddy".

"Dad wasn't a dirty old man," his son said. "Dad was just trying to help somebody and look what he got, and now she's getting three meals a day and a warm place to sleep."

The defense would later bring up the fact that he once pulled a knife on his son Russell during a temper tantrum. Towery would have a history with prostitutes (according to court testimony). Connie Baker would be a prostitute from the 1980s to 1997 and stated that Towery was one of her clients. Baker would also claim Tower as a client but she also had a history of drug possession and auto theft. Diana Wheeler would also admit to being one of Towery's prostitutes in the years of 1994 and 1995. She had come to his home and he even went so far as to clean the stains off his Mel Mac dinnerware. But Wheeler also had a long criminal history like Baker, arrested for prostitution, criminal trespass and giving false identification to a police officer.

The controversy at the trial was if Brittany and Towery had an ongoing "sex-for-money" relationship.

This would be vigorously discounted by family members.

His daughter-in-law would come to the home and help with some housekeeping. His sons would also visit daily and never report any "ladies of the evening" coming to visit their father.

The picture just didn't fit.

Brittany stated she was sent to Towery's place by a fellow streetwalker who went by the moniker of "Green Eyes" but that it was later revealed that no such prostitute by that name existed. Brittany had lied like she had so many times before.

The two seemed to have met by chance.

COMING BACK FROM THE GROCERY STORE

November 13th, 1996 was another normal day for the 80-year old A.B Towery. He had just purchased groceries at an Albertson's store and was walking back to his apartment. As he entered the courtyard, he was approached by the 23-year old Brittany Holberg.

She asked to use his telephone and Towery consented. He wanted to help the sweet-voiced Brittany and didn't believe that she posed any kind of physical threat to him.

What he didn't know was that Brittany was coming down from a cocaine high and had not slept in ten days.

"Brittany could be persuasive," Orange said. "She was well-versed in how to charm people, she knew exactly what to say and do in terms of body language. She was like a trained actress. It didn't take much cajoling on her part to convince Towery to let her inside his home. He probably thought 'what's the big deal?'"

Once inside, Brittany would demand money from the elderly man but he refused. Brittany then attacked Towery, trying to strong arm the wallet out of his pocket. The struggle began in the living room. The two then pushed and pulled each other around a partition that separated the kitchen from the living room. They then returned to the living room. At some point, Towery tried to leave the apartment but Brittany pulled him back in. The evidence also indicated that the two paused during this 45-minute fight, catching their breath and nursing their wounds. Brittany would sustain minor stab wounds to her stomach and thigh.

"This was most likely a fight that had a lot of clutching and grabbing," Orange said. "There was less blood in the living room so the conjecture is that is where the fight started. There was blood near the door so that suggests that Towery was bleeding out and trying to escape for help. Remember, he was a slow-moving 80-year old man. Brittany was a young woman but she was fueled by cocaine. He's getting tired a lot faster than she will."

Eventually, Brittany gained the upper hand. She used various objects around the home to beat down Towery. She started with a cast iron frying pan, then a steam iron, a claw hammer, a fruit knife, a butcher knife and then two forks. Towery would fall to the floor, a bloody mess.

Brittany then took a lamp and shoved its base five inches down his throat which choked him to death.

Satisfied that he had finally killed Tower, Brittany removed her bloody clothes. She washed up in his bathroom then went to his closet to find some clothes that fit her.

Walking back to his dead body, Brittany retrieved the wallet out of Towery's pocket. She took out the $1400 dollars he had and dropped the now empty wallet onto his stomach.

Brittany casually walked out of the apartment and hitched a ride with a young couple. The couple dropped her off at a local crack house where Brittany paid them off with two $100 bills (which had blood stains on them). Inside the drug den, Brittany befriended the proprietor and changed clothes again. She then went to a local hotel with hundreds of dollars worth of cocaine and indulged.

TRIAL

Brittany's defense attorney, Catherine Brown Dodson, would argue that Holberg acted in self-defense when she killed Towery. Her primary argument was that Towery was far from an innocent, elderly man. He was, in fact, a drug abuser himself who became physically violent with Brittany when he found a crack pipe on her person. He then hit Brittany two times in the head when she turned her back to him. Brittany retaliated and ultimately put the lamp post in his mouth in an attempt to end the fight.

Brittany then fled as she believed that no one would believe her side of the story because she was both a prostitute and a drug addict.

While in jail, Brittany would try to coerce Katina Dixon, her cellmate to kill Vickie Marie Kirkpatrick who was the prosecution witness.

Towery's history with prostitutes would be brought up in court testimony. They would also mention incidents of violence with his ex-wife and children but jurors didn't believe the old man was in any type of shape to employ the service of a prostitute.

"My father didn't even like the word 'sex'", one of his sons said. "He was old-fashioned."

A psychiatrist would testify, however, that Brittany had battered wife syndrome, post-traumatic stress disorder, and cocaine addiction.

The jury did not take long to deliberate, finding Brittany to be a cunning, manipulative liar who committed one of the most brutal crimes in the history of Amarillo.

They would find her guilty and Brittany would be moved to death row at Gatesville, Texas.

"I can't even explain to you," Brittany said in a magazine interview. "What it's like to have someone say 'You are sentenced to die.' It's words. You feel helpless, numb. It's almost as if your emotions shut you down."

Brittany would spend her first few weeks in prison laying prone on her bed in a zombie-like state. Over time, she grew accepting of her situation. She knew she was going to die but made it a point to learn to take each day one step at a time.

Her inspiration for cleaning up her act came from the memory of her daughter Mackenzie.

"I cannot live," Brittany said. "And I cannot die, knowing that my child has to live with the horror that these people tried to say about me, the story of the crime, their depiction that I was a cold-blooded person."

Brittany states that she dedicates her days to reading, writing to family and working on her law appeals. She also is anti-death penalty advocate.

She would follow other Texas inmates who were now on death row and make appeals on their behalf, specifically that of Betty Lou Beets.

"I realized," Brittany said. "It doesn't matter whether I'm guilty or innocent, this has now become a very political thing... At this point, they're just killing to kill."

She complained that after a recent jail uprising, the treatment of death row inmates has worsened.

"You would not believe the treatment we are given," Brittany said. "Just two weeks ago, we were informed that not only would we be strip-searched for our one hour of recreation a day, but also when taken for a shower. So for the last two weeks, we have been stripped no less than six times a day. This is every day, sometimes at times like 2:30-3 a.m., and we never leave the building or our cells for that matter."

As of this writing, Brittany's stay of execution has been appealed and appealed for the past eighteen years.

Her attorneys would exhaust the appeal process in the state system but it is now in the federal courts.

Her case, however, has been costing taxpayers "conservatively to be at least $400,000" according to county criminal attorney James Farren. In the future, he has decided to forgo seeking the death penalty in capital cases.

Farren continues to favor a death penalty but only under certain circumstances like "a guy walks into a day care center and kills the children or if someone kills a police officer or a firefighter in the line of duty."

Farren predicted that Brittany would remain on death row for another five years at least. "They can go through the U.S District Court in Amarillo, then it can go to the Fifth U.S Circuit Court and the U.S. Supreme Court. Then from there it can go back to the U.S. District."

But the appeals can come to a halt if the district judge refuses to hear it again.

"If the Supreme Court says 'no'," Farren said. "That's when the district judge can feel safe in stopping this process."

The entire process has been an infuriating one for the Towery family. His son both rages and mourns about what happened to his father.

"She tried to apologize to us during the trial," Russel Towery said. " I got up and walked out. I'm sure other families are going through the same things I'm going through. It's been almost 19 years ... people forget."

"I don't want to die before she does. I want to stand there as she's kicking and screaming going to the death gurney. I want her to think about what my dad went through when she didn't even know his name," he said. "She thinks that because she said she was sorry, that everything's all right. ... she is evil and needs to be destroyed."

HUSBAND KILLER : THE TRUE STORY OF TRACEY GRISSOM

89

Claiming to be a victim of rape and other abuses, a distraught Tracey Grissom would travel to her ex-husband Hunter's workplace and shoot him six times in the back, receiving a twenty-five-year life sentence for his murder.

Her defense attorney would argue that Tracey was motivated by post-traumatic stress disorder caused by her Hunter's constant abuse and sexual assaults. One jury member had even asked the judge to be lenient in her sentencing as they were not allowed to hear details of her Hunter's alleged abuses (beatings, rape, sodomy).

But what really happened in the years that led up to May 15th, 2012? Was she in fact the victim of years of abuse by a psychotic husband? Or did she want to cash in on his $100,000 life insurance policy?

INSTANT ATTRACTION

The couple would meet during a dinner party in 2003 in Tuscaloosa, Alabama. Tracey was twenty-one years old and going through a divorce. She had a son, James Michael, from the previous marriage.

Family and friends would describe the union as "love at first sight." Hunter was blown away by the young Tracey's blue eyes and facial beauty.

"For him, it was love at first sight," crime author William Phelps said. "She was gorgeous."

A whirlwind courtship would ensue and the couple would elope in 2004.

"In the beginning, it was good," Tracey told CBS' 48 hours. "We had a friendship. Just your normal, honeymoon phase marriage."

"He was fun," Tracey said. "And he was attractive."

Hunter was two years younger than Tracey, however, and his mother felt that he had jumped the gun too early in the relationship.

Her words proved to be prophetic as after only eight months into the marriage, the marriage went south.

According to Tracey, their marital problems began with Hunter's drug addiction.

"I had caught him smoking marijuana," Tracey said. "Doing illegal things could cause a problem and I couldn't risk losing my son over."

Tracey claimed that she threatened her new spouse with a divorce but Hunter gave her his word that he would stop with his drug use. She stated that the relationship improved and the decided to start a construction company together.

"I took out an equity line to start a company," Tracey said. "Which was Grissom Construction. It was all in my name."

Hunter specialized in building elaborate boat docks. He had an artistic eye and could do docks, stairs, and other accouterments. The business began to grow in short order.

"They're going to take on the world," Phelps said. "They're going to be entrepreneurs and they're gonna make it."

They then had a daughter of their own, Anna Grace. The child was a long time coming for the couple. They had been trying for a long time as Tracey had five miscarriages before Anna Grace was born.

"She was premature," Tracey recalled. "Her heart and lungs were not developed. A very stressful time."

Behind closed doors things were rocky. On the surface, however, things looked good. They had a young family and were making money.

"All-American family," Phelps said. "White-picket fence. The whole nine yards. Middle-class. Suburbia. Maybe the Prince Charming that she's been waiting for."

But again, this was only on the surface. Tracey harbored secrets of her own. One of which was her own addiction to prescription drugs.

"Psychologically, there's something going on here," Phelps said. "There's something going on behind those beautiful eyes and it ain't good."

Tracey would often turn on on the children, showing off her temper. Then she would turn on Hunter.

"This would cause friction in the marriage," Phelps said. "And where there's friction, there's fire."

SETTING THE STAGE

Tracey would later state that Hunter would "act strangely" shortly before she filed divorce. She was a registered nurse and gave him an over-the-counter drug test. According to her, Hunter tested posted for marijuana, Oxycontin, opiates, and methamphetamine.

Hunter would later be arrested for marijuana possession but his family would insist that he never did the harder drugs.

Tracey would file for divorce in the summer of 2010 after six years of marriage. According to her, this would prompt physical abuse from Hunter.

Hunter had to move out but their divorce agreement would allow him access to the home.

"In September of 2010," Tracey recalled. "That was the first time he physically hit me. It (the abuse) got progressively worse. He had made the comments that if I told anybody he would kill me. I believed him."

Hunter' co-workers and family members would have a different take on the situation, however. His co-workers remembered a time when she tracked him down at one of the jobs and made a scene.

"She's screaming, jumping on him," Hunter's co-worker said. "Said something about him having another girlfriend and used the expression about, 'You are mine. I'll kill you. I'll kill you. You are mine."

"She's borderline demonic," Hunter's mother said. " mean, I absolutely believe—that she is that troubled."

Hunter's family continued to believe that he did not abuse Tracey.

"He did not have an abusive, an angry bone in his body," Hunter's aunt Gina said. "In fact, we kind of laughed at him because he was too laid-back."

The divorce was finalized in October of 2010.

EVIDENCE OF ABUSE?

Loran Richards was the first of Tracey's friends to notice the minor injuries on her body. She would inquire about the bruises but the answers she received were always evasive. Seeing Tracey with a black eye, however, forced her to try and get more answers.

"I said, Tracey, you may have terrible luck," Richards recalled. "But nobody is so unlucky that they trip, fall down the stairs, and hit their face on a baseball in the eye socket. So don't give me a lame excuse. You don't have to give me any excuse, but let's take a picture."

Tracey broke down. She gave her friend all of the grisly details, detailing the abuse she suffered at the hands of Hunter. Loran then became her advocate, taking pictures of Tracey's injuries. She would later state that she saw blood stains and other signs of abuse at Tracey's home.

THAT FATEFUL NIGHT

Now divorced, Hunter would arrive at Tracey's home on November 22nd, 2010.

According to Tracey, he then became enraged when Tracey told him that she had spent the night with a new lover.

"He told me that he was gonna kill me," Tracey recalled. Tracey stated that she tried to escape, running into the closet in order to "get away from the kids and to pray." Tracey's eleven-year-old son from a previous relationship was in the home as was the four-year-old daughter they have together.

Hunter caught up with her and knocked her to the ground. He tied a belt around her ankles and then began choking her.

Half-conscious, Tracey alleged to have been raped and sodomized.

The brutal attack would leave Tracey unconscious. She would wake up the next morning on the bathroom floor.

"I called Hunter," Tracey recalled. "I told him that I was bleeding and that I was hurt and that I needed help. And he told me, 'Fuck you. I hope you die."

Tracey wound up in the emergency room after the attack. Hospital records would show that she had a laceration on her head, bruises, and ligature marks on her feet.

Tracey would then be referred to the Turning Point domestic violence center.

Marian Waters would describe Tracey's injuries as among the worst she had ever seen in a twenty-year career.

Waters would testify that Tracey had suffered a horrific assault. She described her mental state as typical of someone who had just been raped; fearful, jumpy, fearing for her life.

Tracey had suffered a hematoma on her side that was the side of a grapefruit. She also claimed to have experienced rectal nerve damage which would require surgery as well as torn vaginal muscles requiring her to have a hysterectomy.

Police were called and Hunter would be arrested for rape, sodomy, kidnapping and domestic violence.

"And at that point, I feared for my life," Tracey recalled. "And I feared for my children's life."

A HIDDEN AGENDA

Hunter would be freed on bail but Tracey got a restraining order against him. She bought a gun and did not go anywhere unarmed.

She took photos of her injuries on the night of the alleged attack and texted them to Loran. Later, they would take more pictures.

Angered, Hunter would stop paying her spousal and child support. Tracey, however, may have had another scenario in mind for obtaining money.

She had forced Hunter to take out a $103,000 life insurance policy around the time their daughter was born.

On May 24, 2012, the day before Tracey shot Hunter, she would place a call to MetLife that was recorded.

"Thank you for calling MetLife, this is Pam. May I please have your name?"

"Tracey Grissom."

Tracey would then explain that she was angry that her husband stopped making payments on his policy. During their divorce proceedings, he had agreed to continue paying the premiums. Tracey stated she was calling to make sure that they had the correct address on file.

"Is there anything else I can do for you today?

"That's gonna be it!" Tracey said, hanging up.

"Well, May 14th was just like any other day," Tracey said, explaining the call to the insurance company. "However, I had moved four different times. Me and my children were running. We were running from Hunter. So I had called the company to let them know that they had my old address and to make an address change."

FALSE RAPE?

Shelly Standridge was hired by Hunter to defend him in the rape case. She would state that Hunter denied raping or even assaulting Tracey that night. Hunter did, however, admit to the fact that he and his wife had consensual sex that night...Rough consensual sex.

"So that night," Standridge said. "Hunter said that she was depressed and claiming she was going to kill herself. She was saying she wanted their relationship to work."

So she undressed in front of him. Her beauty was always impossible for Hunter to resist.

The two had sex despite Hunter having a new girlfriend at home.

Hunter's aunt, Gina, believed that Tracey wanted to kill Hunter before the rape case went to court.

"He had a new girlfriend, he was living with her," Phelps said. "He was moving on with his life. Hunter would claim that Tracey was jealous, obsessive, even stalked them."

"Hunter had moved on," Hunter's aunt said. "There was some court dates coming up that would prove that Hunter was innocent. There were court dates coming up that he would get visitation to his daughter. She had a lot to lose."

Tracey was on the anti-anxiety drug Klonopin. Hunter would tell his attorney that Tracey would take more than her prescribed dose. Because of this, she fell and cut her head. Hunter would then leave the house around 10:30 pm and go to his father's house. Tracey would call him hours later, at 3:20 am.

Hunter would state that Tracey had called to threaten him. She told him if he didn't want the responsibility of the children then she would make it where he would never be able to see them again.

Hunter's attorney did not know what Tracey's motive was for crying rape. She was very upset that he had a girlfriend.

MORE LIES...

Hunter would be arrested nearly twelve hours later, to his total shock.

Tracey would give her side of the story to the police which later is proven to be false.

She would tell police that Hunter had thrown her against the bathtub around 10 pm and claim to be unconscious until 4 am the next morning.

"But her phone records show she was on the phone all night, so she was never unconscious," Standridge said. "She was also using her data at 10:42 that night. She was using it again at 10:50 that night. ... She sends a text to her boyfriend at 1:49 am. She sends a text to her friend at 2:07 am. She sends another text to her boyfriend at 2:07 am."

Tracey would blame the calls on Hunter.

"All I do know is I was not the only person using my phone that night," Tracey said, suggesting that Hunter used her phone.

Medical records would show that Tracey's head wound was "purely superficial".

Only one suture was needed.

Furthermore, there was nothing on the medical record to support the fact that Tracey experienced vaginal and rectal tears. She did have bruises on her ankle and legs but the photos taken by police at the emergency room would not resemble the same photos that Tracey and her friend Loran would take days later. In the photos taken at the emergency room, an area of Tracey's body has no bruises. Days later, there is discoloration.

Tracey's attorney would blame the discrepancy on "blood thinners" which would cause Tracey to bruise easily.

There was also a discrepancy in her phone records. She would take a photo of her inner thigh, a deep bruise. This area of her body was not photographed by police during her emergency room visit. But on December 9th, almost two weeks later, Tracey took a photo of her inner thigh with the deep bruise

"He (Hunter) told me that he would make it to where nobody would ever want me," Tracey said after a 2010 attack. "I didn't report it because I thought he would kill me."

THE FINAL STRAW

Tracey woke up pissed on May 15th, 2012.

Hunter had been ordered to pay $2,100 a month for the rest of his life. He was not complying with the court order claiming that he was "out of work."

Tracey stated that she was on her way to a job interview when she saw a Grissom Construction sign out of the corner of her eye.

She stated that her initial plan was to take a photograph of Hunter at the job site in order to show proof that he was working as part of her litigation.

"I was getting ready to take the picture and when I looked up he was standing almost directly towards the front of the boat trailer," Tracey said. "He was looking back directly at me. He had this face, that's like mean - just, I don't know how to describe it. I mean, I see it over and over like it's right there all the time. He flipped me the bird, which to me was kinda like, 'Yeah I'm workin. Screw you.' And at that point, I panicked. At that point, I didn't know what else to do except to defend myself."

Tracey started firing. The first shot hit Hunter in the arm. He started to run and she fired again repeatedly. One of the bullets punctured Hunter's heart and he died of massive internal bleeding.

William Dockery was working with Hunter and was an eyewitness to the shooting. Hunter had turned to Dockery before the shooting and told him to "call the law". Before Dockery could pick up his cell phone, Tracey had commenced shooting.

Tracey then pulled out her own cell phone and called the cops on herself. She tearfully described that she had just murdered her husband.

CONFESSION

Tracey told detectives exactly what was going through her mind when she came upon Hunter at the construction site.

"Tell me about what happened," the detective said. "What led up to...what's going on."

"In November of 2010, he beat me unconscious and raped me...and, and left me for dead....and, and I finally pressed charges against him and he told me that he would make my life a living hell...and that's what he's done."

"What, what happened this morning that led up to you going..."

"I was going to work and I saw him...and he's been claiming that he-he's not working. And, so I pulled in there to take a picture of him...cause it was the truck that's still in my name...and the boat that's still in my name...and the trailer that's still in my name...He just stared at me and flipped me off...and I just went in there and shot him...I just shot him, I shot him, and I shot him."

Tracey would be distraught and tearful during her interrogation room confession. A few weeks later, however, she would call the insurance company to let them know that Hunter had died.

"Well, I was actually calling because I didn't know what I needed to do ... Hunter passed away May 15th and I actually am going a court case right now because it was due to self-defense..."

Hunter's family went ballistic over this. Tracey would claim that she had no money but she continued to pay his life insurance premiums.

"Even through the times when she's screamin' that she's destitute and has no money ... she continued to pay life insurance premium," Hunter's mother said.

"I don't think my sister concocted a story," Tracey's sister said. "Just so she could get insurance money. ... But that's all they (the prosecution) had."

THE TRIAL

Tracey's allegations of rape and sodomy would not be allowed in court testimony. She was allowed, however, to detail the effects of Hunter's abuse on her were.

Taking the stand, Tracey would lift up her shirt in court and show herself wearing a colostomy bag. She stated that she had undergone several surgeries after her husband's daily rapes wherein she suffered permanent rectal and vaginal damage.

Hunter's family was then allowed to speak at the hearing.

"This tremendous loss has changed me," Hunter's mother, Melanie Garner said. "And I don't know how to change back."

Chloe, Hunter's sister, had a victim's services officer read her letter in court.

"Tracey is psychotic," Chloe wrote. "She is the most selfish person human being on this earth."

"Every mother should pray every night that your son doesn't fall in love with someone like Tracey," Hunter's aunt, Gina Grissom said. "There have been lots of allegations against Hunter. We've never believed anything that has come out of her (Tracey's) mouth."

His aunt then looked directly at Tracey.

"Hunter was proud of his name. Why would you still choose to use our name, and bring it down?" suggesting that if Tracey hated him so much why didn't she go revert to her maiden name after the divorce.

The jurors would find Tracey guilty of murder. She would be sentenced to twenty-five years in prison.

One of the jurors, Janice Kelly, would contact Grissom's attorney Warren Freeman the morning after the trial. She had remorse over her decision and said that she wouldn't have convicted her had they had the rapes and abuse allegations been introduced as evidence.

"I feel I made a mistake," Kelly said. "If I had to do it over again, we'd have had a hung jury. We didn't get her side. She did not get a fair trial."

"We voted to convict because there was no dispute that Tracey shot Hunter," the jury foreman wrote in a letter that was addressed in the courthouse. "Jurors didn't believe prosecutor claims that she did it in order to collect a life insurance policy. We felt the shooting was a crime of passion, not for financial gain and that she should be sentenced accordingly. I wish we had seen evidence of the rape allegation. We feel that she just 'lost it.'"

"It's not fair, it's not fair!" Tracey sobbed as she was led out of the courthouse and to jail.

"We think the sentencing was too harsh," Tracey's attorney Warren Freeman said. "Considering you have the foreperson of the jury actually saying, we don't feel like she should be punished according to being found guilty of murder. Let's just say that there will be a basis for a new trial, and part of it will be something that the jurors saw that they weren't supposed to see and I'm going to just leave it at that until I file my motion."

"My son died running for his life," Hunter's mother said. "I don't know what was running through his mind but I hear him say 'momma.'"

"People who think that I murdered him in cold blood," Tracey said. "Either don't know the whole story or don't know everything that's happened.

Tracey was asked on CBS' 48 hours if she regretted pulling the trigger on that fateful day.

"No," she said flatly. "Because if I hadn't I would be dead. I truly believe that."

"She has a way of making everything she does look right," Hunter's aunt, Gina scoffed.

AMBER CUMMINGS

On the surface, James and Amber Cummings had it all.

They had been married for twelve years. James had inherited millions of dollars from his father and they owned a home in the peaceful, seaside town of Belfast, Maine.

"On paper, they were a couple that looked as if they had everything," forensic psychologist Paula Orange said. "Definitely one of those cases where looks are more than deceiving. They are downright deadly."

The couple met in Fort Bragg, California. Amber was a tall brunette while James was overweight and had an awkward vibe about him.

Amber found him charming, however, and would later describe him as the "nicest guy she'd ever met." She would marry him at 19 years of age and things looked bright for the young couple until Amber got pregnant.

"That is when his personality started to change," Orange said. "He would drive away Amber's family members in California and seek to keep her isolated. This brought much consternation to Amber's side of the family, obviously. There was one heart-breaking instance where Amber's mother and sister went to a neighbor's yard just to get a glimpse of Amber's daughter riding her tricycle."

James wanted no outside influence on Amber or their daughter so he began moving the family around. They left California when Amber turned five and moved to Texas. Then they traveled the country in a motor home until 2007 when the finally settled in Belfast, Maine.

"My husband said that he hated people and that he didn't care where we moved," Amber said. "I always wanted to live in a nice, small town in Maine."

EARLY LIFE

James' life seemed to have been one of trouble even though he was born into wealth.

His father would be murdered by one of his former employees in 1997 which was preceded by James making headline news as he videotaped his own mother doing heroin.

James would have numerous run-ins with the law himself.

"He had a bunch of assault charges," Orange said. "Some were cases where he was the victim. Others were cases where he was the perpetrator. When he was the perp, his father's money always bailed him out."

According to some Internet rumors, James' father had allegedly injured himself while getting off a forklift on one of the docks in the Fort Bragg harbor, breaking his knee in the fall.

Cummings then went to a friend's house and fell to the ground outside claiming that he "tripped in a hole." James' father then sued the owners of the property and won.

"That gives you an idea of the kind of guy James' father was," Orange said. "Rumors abound on the internet and in the Fort Bragg community about how he acquired his wealth. None of it is verifiable aside from the fact that the majority of the trust is funneled through a trailer park, which is odd."

Cummings Sr. would own many businesses and it would be one of his employees, a man named Williams Vargas who would gun him down.

Vargas detonated a homemade bomb he called a "firecracker" outside Cummings' home. The disgruntled employee then panicked as one of Cummings' neighbors drove by and blocked his escape. Cummings Sr. then came out with his own gun to investigate the blast which shattered his window.

Vargas then pulled out his own gun and shot Cummings. He had been working for Cummings at the Noyo Harbor trailer park and was allowed to live there in exchange for labor. But he began having problems with other residents which he would blame Cummings Sr. for.

Cummings, 77 years old at the time of his murder, had built his wealth by running restaurants, motels, a fish-processing plant as well as trailer parks. He also owned the Depot Mall shopping center and a McDonald's restaurant.

``Jim was quite an entrepreneur. He had quite a lot of land holdings, in some key areas, really, in the harbor and other areas around," former City Manager Gary Milliman said.

James Jr. would be the beneficiary of his father's death. He would tell people that he made his living "selling off Texas real estate" but the truth was that he was a trust fund kid living off the businesses that his father created.

The trust fund started off by giving Jams a whopping ten million dollars a year. The funds would deplete rapidly, however, as James would have a six-year legal battle against trustees whom he thought were mismanaging the money.

His mental illness would grow worse as his finances decreased.

NEO-NAZI SYMPATHIES

"He would go on daily rants about Barack Obama," Orange said. "Which would seem harmless at first until Amber realized that James was, in fact, a white supremacist. He began spending his days hunting down rare Nazi artifacts on the Internet and purchasing them."

James had applied to the National Socialist Movement, one of the largest neo-Nazi clubs in the country. He had written numerous white supremacy organizations on-line and began to mix toxic chemicals in their kitchen sink while telling Amber about his desire to make a "dirty bomb."

James had hired a pair of contractors to paint the interior of the house. The painters would later testify to witnessing James berate his wife. He would tell the men about his guns and go on about Adolf Hitler.

Thinking he had an eager audience, James bragged about his collection of silverware and plate settings that he claimed to have been used by Hitler himself.

"Check this out," James showed a swastika flag to the painter. "This was real. Not a knock-off. They actually waved this same flag while Hitler spoke."

James would run his household as if he were Hitler himself, marching around the home wearing a black hat and uniform with a Nazi armband.

Working himself up into a Nazi-like frenzy of rage, he would then abuse Amber physically, emotionally and sexually.

"He stripped away whatever self-esteem she had," Orange said. "He had no friends himself and didn't allow her to have any either."

As the years went by, James developed paranoid schizophrenic tendencies which had given birth to ideas that grew more bizarre with time. The married couple slept in separate bedrooms and James had guns placed under both of their pillows "just in case."

On one occasion, Amber left the home for an extended period of time. James immediately became enraged upon her arrival back. He demanded to know where she was and who she was with. Amber had gone to meet with a home-schooling group which they both previously agreed would be a good idea.

James went ballistic, berating Amber and throwing his sharpened Nazi knives against the wall.

CHILD ABUSE

James did not limit his abuse to Amber. His paranoid anger soon extended to their daughter, Clara.

This became evident to Amber when their daughter had come across James' collection of Nazi knives and began examining them.

"Leave those alone!" James screamed as he ran into the room and grabbed the box of knives away from the girl. "These belonged to the Führer! The Führer!"

Amber had very little self-esteem left, but she intervened when James would physically abuse their daughter. She would throw herself between the two and take the beating herself.

This would only incite James further as the would beat Amber then march up to Clara's room and continue his abuse.

"He kept them isolated and feeling helpless," Orange said. "They tried to escape on a few occasions but he caught them, keeping them locked in the house. She thought he had some kind of superhuman power."

CHILD PORNOGRAPHY

Seeking new outlets, James' mind became so perverted that he soon began indulging in child pornography. He showed his collection to Amber who shuddered in horror.

"Which one do you like best?" he would ask his wife, pointing to a series of pictures on the scream.

In addition to the child pornography, James began teaching his daughter to see the world through his racist viewpoint.

"This is equal-opportunity hatred," he preached to his daughter. "We can hate everybody."

"He was deluded," Orange said. "He actually saw himself as the second coming of Hitler. He began seeing his daughter as his future helper, someone who would be in charge of 'reconditioning' women and children after he declared war on the United States."

James wanted to build a torture chamber in the basement of the house. He told Amber about his desire to kill people and "peel the skin off their bones." He also obsessed on the Showtime television series, "Dexter", which featured a serial killer as the protagonist. James would then take long walks around the Belfast area, daydreaming about living out his 'Dexter' fantasy.

"He constantly talked about the different ways of killing and torturing people and hiding their bodies," Amber said. "He used to say it was a need in him."

THE FINAL STRAW

"The abuse happened incrementally for her," Orange said. "It is easy to sit back and judge a person like her, saying that she should have just left. But she was like a frog in a pot of cool water before it starts to boil. The abuse started small at first then bit by bit it increased as her self-esteem diminished. But when it came to protecting her daughter, she had to act."

One December 9th, 2008, Amber Cummings finally had enough.

She got up like she normally did after another night of abuse by her husband.

"Amber discovered James messing around with the chemicals in the kitchen," Orange said. "He said that he would bury her in the backyard if he said anything."

She sent her daughter downstairs to eat breakfast while she pulled out a .45 caliber pistol from underneath her pillow.

Then she held the gun underneath her own throat.

"Amber's first thought was to kill herself," Orange said. "But then she saw her daughter's doll in the room. She shuddered to think of her daughter spending the rest of her childhood with her father as she realized that it was only a matter of time before James' obsession with child pornography would make him do something to Clara. So she had to seek an alternative course of action."

Amber would later tell court-appointed psychologists that James' infatuation with child pornography and his "sexual attraction to young girls" made her believe that he was becoming obsessed with their daughter.

Fueled by her protective maternal instinct, Amber entered the bedroom where James was sleeping. She never had any gumption to stand up for herself when James abused her.

But when it came to protecting her daughter, a whole new Amber showed up.

She pointed the gun at the back of James' head and fired. Blood splattered against the bedpost. Shocked by her own display of violence, Amber sprinted down the steps and ordered her daughter to go to her neighbor's and stay there.

"If it wasn't for my daughter, I would have committed suicide years ago," Amber said. "Some of the mental torture will never leave me the rest of my life. It was so severe, it will be with me every day."

Amber then called the police and told them what she did.

"It's hard for us to justify shooting somebody who's asleep in the bed," Sheriff Jeffrey Trafton said. "But when we arrived she looked more like a victim than a killer."

"She was in a state of shock," Orange said. "She had finally taken action to free herself from years of abuse. The state, of course, cannot let such a deed go unchecked."

A CONSPIRACY AFOOT?

As police investigated the murder scene, they discovered another James Cummings secret.

He was gathering materials to make a "dirty bomb."

Fueled by his white supremacist ideology, James planned to go to Washington, D.C for Barack Obama's presidential inauguration. Once there, he would set off his dirty bomb.

"He had all the ingredients inside the garage," Orange said. "The FBI found the instructions for the dirty bomb. There were four 1-gallon containers with uranium, thorium and beryllium powder. There were numerous other jugs which contained lithium metal, thermite, magnesium ribbon, black iron oxide and other explosive substances. James Cummings meant business and there is clear evidence he was going to follow through on his plan. Whether he could have pulled it off is another story."

Had his plan gone to fruition, James could have potentially killed hundreds of people.

Amber saved not only herself but innumerable lives by killing James herself.

"The stuff that he had wasn't dangerous," Bangor Police Chief Jeffrey Trafton said. "In its present form, it wasn't dangerous to the community. Technicians told me what you had to do, you had to get real close for a long period of time before it would have any effect as far as the radioactivity. When the stuff was found, obviously detectives from the state police came and we didn't know what it was. But there was no danger to the community. That was established fairly quickly. But my involvement since it was handed over to the state police has been little to none."

THE TRIAL

Amber would remain in a state of shock after the murder. She worried more about her daughter's well-being than her own. She was fully prepared to go to jail.

"Her mental state was still askew after she killed James," Orange said. "She probably saw prison as a welcome respite from her abusive life. She had been in 'prison' already and saw the jail system as a safe place."

Amber would plead guilty during trial proceedings. Her story would make the media rounds, however, and she soon found numerous supporters in her small Maine town. People showed up wearing "Free Amber" t-shirts.

"There was no way in hell a jury in that vicinity would have found her guilty," Orange said. "None."

Amber seemed to have found leniency on both sides of the judicial system. Her attorney and the prosecutors would come up with a plea deal which called for a sentence of up to eight years but with Amber serving no less than a year. This would be followed by six years of probation.

Her attorney then recommended to the judge that Amber spend no whatsoever behind bars while the Assistant Attorney General, Leane Zania, wanted Cummings to spend a year in jail.

"This kind of 'self-help' is severely anti-social behavior," Zania wrote. "It will be punished accordingly."

During the course of the trial, Amber would not take the stand in her defense. Three mental health experts who had counseled her after the killing all affirmed the fact that Amber had endured traumatic abuse. They advised the judge not to send her to jail.

The psychiatrists had given Amber a diagnosis of "shared psychotic disorder" which in layman's terms meant that she had absorbed some of his craziness just by being around him.

"You don't hang out by the outhouse without getting a rash," Orange said. "So that is how Amber was able to endure all of that psychological trauma. She became so desensitized to it that it became the norm after a few years."

The judge sentenced her to eight years in prison but it was a suspended sentence, allowing her to go free.

"The terrible thing is, I was forced to take the life of someone that I loved very much to save my daughter that I love very much," Amber said. "It's something that I will have to live with for the rest of my life, and it won't be easy. I'll always wonder. I'll always be looking over my shoulder, always wondering if he can come back from the dead."

In her public remarks, Amber requested that the community forgive her husband and not have any anger toward him.

"I just want to thank the community and people of Maine," Amber said after leaving the courtroom. "Because without them, I don't think my daughter and I could have made all this progress. Really, really wonderful caring people. If I was anywhere else, we wouldn't be doing this well. I believe that with all my heart."

"The people around here are pretty incredible. They gave me the benefit of the doubt, and a chance to prove myself. There was a lot of support, an unbelievable amount of support, in Belfast. People came out and took care of us and made sure we had everything we need."

Amber stated that after she shot James that she fell into a "state of shock and numbness." She would continue to dream about James, having nightmares about him choking her.

Since then, she dedicated herself to trying to undo the mental damage James did to her daughter.

"I hope to raise a really good kid, who cares a lot about people," Amber said. I hope she ends up strong and can take care of herself. I think she will."

DEATH ROW GRANNY

It never ends.

No way.

No way am I letting this man demean and degrade me another day.

He's just like my father.

A binge drinker. And the binges were happening more and more.

He's on the road to nowhere and taking me with him.

It never ends.

First my father. Now him.

Fuck it.

I threw the cigarette on the blanket. I knew it was flammable.

Then I watched the smoke rise and smiled.

In Lumberton, North Carolina, Thomas Burke fell victim to a house fire which was caused by a burning cigarette. Investigative authorities thought that he had fallen asleep while smoking, leaving thirty-eight-year-old Velma Burke as his widow.

They didn't know that the fire was set by Velma.

Velma knew how to play the part of the grieving widow. She cried and gave the authorities the requisite crocodile tears. No one would believe that the murder of Thomas

Burke would set off a series of killings performed by the seemingly kind and harmless church-going woman with the soft voice.

EARLY LIFE

Velma Bullard grew up as the second of nine children in the rural part of Sampson County, North Carolina.

Times were tough for the Bullard family. They would live on a small farm with no electricity, running water or an outhouse.

"They had to go outdoors," forensic psychologist Paula Orange said. "The entire family had to endure the indignity of going into the woods or using pots to shit and piss."

The home was small and cramped for the nine children. Velma would be forced to sleep in the same bedroom with her parents until the age of five.

Her father was a loom repairman (fixing an apparatus that was used to weave clothing) and an abusive alcoholic. Velma had an older brother, Olive, who were subject to his nightly beatings. Lillie, her mother, was too meek to protect her children from her husband's violent outbursts.

"She had the type of father who would not need any provocation," Orange said. "He would take out the pettiest frustrations, like not being able to find something around the house, and take it out on the children. Velma would become resentful toward her mother who was too weak or indifferent to stop her father from beating on the kids. She accepted his discipline as 'the way it was.'"

Velma would find school as a welcome escape from her dreadful home life. She loved her teacher and was an excellent student during her early grade school years. When she would return home from school, she took solace in the fact that her father would always arrive home late as he worked long hours at the textile mill.

"Her father Murphy had that Protestant work ethic in him," Orange said. "He accepted the long hours and low pay, seeing a kind of nobility in that. Only problem was, he would binge drink. Not store bought alcohol but homemade moonshine. After a couple of shots, he would be 'lit' and inflict his wrath on everyone in the house."

By the age of eleven, Velma would be forced to take on various chores around the farm. She would clean up the house, washing and iron everyone's clothing (eleven people). Her father would chastise her for not mending or sewing his work clothes properly as well.

"Her father was a stern taskmaster," Orange said. "Hell, you can say 'slave driver.' He would have Velma come home early from school days when the laundry got too backed up. Velma hated this and felt embarrassed. Her family didn't have much and as she grew older her classmates began to see her for what she was, a poor girl that was an easy mark for teasing."

Velma would grow to be 5'3" but gain weight as she got older. She would be mocked about her obesity, her shoddy clothes the gap between her two front teeth. She would also be called "knot head" after she ran head first into a boy at school which left a permanent contusion on her forehead.

By the age of twelve, Velma seemed to have taken on all of her mother's duties. She would cook all of the family meals in addition to performing cleaning around the farm house. She would miss school for days at a time as her father forced her to complete chores around the home before she could continue her education.

"Academic achievement was not at the forefront of her father's mind," Orange said. "Her mother was of little use because of her depression and mental illness. Velma was the oldest girl so she took on the duties of mom at an age where she should have been playing with dolls."

ANGER, ABUSE, AND CHURCH

Despite her father's verbal abuse and alcohol-fueled beatings, the family kept up a face of religious interest. Velma would be sent to Bible school every year until the age of thirteen. During her last year of Bible school, her father marked the occasion by buying Velma a silk pink dress with ribbons. Velma recalled the day as one of the happiest of her life.

The happiness would be short-lived.

Velma would claim that her father raped her when she was thirteen years old. She revealed this only to her pastor in her later years before she stood trial. Velma did not even tell her mother whom she did not think would believe the molestation took place.

"Things that went on inside our home when I grew up," Velma said. "Were kept inside."

At the age of fifteen, Velma continued to excel in school. Despite her chubby physique, she becomes adept at basketball and is pegged to be the team's star player for the upcoming season. But her father did not allow her to play.

"Who is going to iron these damn clothes?" he snarled.

The family then moved to Robeson county and switched from the Presbyterian denomination to Baptist. It was here that Velma would meet Thomas Burke and the two made it clear that they wanted to date. Once again, Velma's father would intervene, telling Velma that she had to wait until her sixteenth birthday until she could date.

The two waited patiently for her birthday to arrive and the following year Thomas would propose to her while they went to the movies.

Knowing that her father would not approve, Velma and Thomas eloped, moving to Dillon, South Carolina. Neither Thomas or Velma had any money as they both quit high school to get married. Thomas then went to work at a local textile mill.

"At this point, I believe that Velma began to realize that her life would not be that much better with Thomas," Orange said. "He literally has the same job as her father."

Economics forced Velma and Thomas to move in with his parents. This arrangement would last for a year until Thomas got a better paying job at a soft drink company.

At the age of nineteen, Velma would give birth to her first son, Ronnie. The couple would then move back to Parkton, North Carolina where they would remain in the same home for eleven years. Two years later, the young couple would welcome a daughter named Kim.

A CYCLE OF RELIGION AND ABUSE

The Burkes would be fixtures at the local Baptist church with Velma taking the reigns to teach a Sunday school class. But the prayers and sermons would do little to offset the growing ennui in the Burke home. Two years after giving birth to Kim, Velma would get hit by a drunk driver while crossing the street. She would be hospitalized for an extended period, suffering both physically and mentally.

Thomas' job at the soft drink company would not be enough to provide for the family. Velma would be forced to leave her small children at home and work in a textile mill just like her father. The couple would have different work hours, with Velma working nights and Thomas working days as they would take turns watching the children.

Velma would fall victim to the hard work at the mill and the stress of raising two young children. She began bleeding and her doctor performed a hysterectomy.

Velma's mother would take pity on the couple and give them one acre of land near their old farm. Thomas would build a three-bedroom home for the family but Velma was already going down a slippery slope. Her personality changed after the hysterectomy, claiming that she always felt "nervous and afraid."

Things would get worse as Thomas suffered a head injury in a car accident. He then began to drink heavily and begin to beat Velma.

"It was deja vu," Orange said. "Velma had, in essence, married her father."

One night, the couple argued and Thomas punched Velma in an alcohol-fueled tantrum. The police are called to the home and Velma sent Thomas to the state hospital to get treatment for his drinking. Her husband remains there for three days but when he returns home, his behavior is worse than behavior. He's angry at Velma for sending him to the "drunk tank". His alcoholism worsens and he would go on to lose his job because of absenteeism.

"Velma is thirty-five years old at this time," Orange said. "But she's an old thirty-five with crow's feet under her eyes and a hangdog look. She's had a rough life, not necessarily by her own design, and it has taken its toll."

Velma leaves the textile mill but then finds two different jobs in order to support the family. During the day, she works as a sales clerk in a Belk department store. At night, she goes to work as a machine operator in a cotton mill.

Thomas, meanwhile, would continue to drink.

He rages on a daily basis, on one occasion he pinned son Ronnie up against the wall and threatened him with a knife. Velma would faint during the encounter and be transported to the hospital. She was diagnosed as having a nervous breakdown and lapsed into a serious depression. The medical staff gave her tranquilizers to calm down. Velma believed that it was during this stint in the hospital that she became addicted to the painkillers.

"The drugs were helping," Orange said. "When nothing else did. So she wanted more and more."

Velma's children acknowledged that their mother's mood swings were due to the drugs.

Over the next three years, Velma would go in and out of the hospital for drug overdoses. After each visit, her addiction only grew as did her prescription list.

"She fell through the cracks in her own family," Orange said. "And in the system itself. Her family had their own issues to deal with as Thomas would abuse everyone on a daily basis. Finally, Velma did something she could control. She killed her husband."

On April 21st, 1969, Velma would drop a cigarette on the floor of her home and waited until her husband inhaled enough smoke to die.

His death, however, would do nothing to solve Velma's problems.

Her addictions and anxiety would only get worse.

A HOSPITAL FREQUENT FLYER

Velma would have another nervous breakdown after killing Thomas and lapse into a guilt-ridden depression. But seven months later, a co-worker at the Belk department store would introduce her to fifty-four-year-old Jennings Barfield. Jennings had emphysema and diabetes but Velma would marry him anyway. Unlike her marriage with Thomas which started out well, Velma's marriage with the older Jennings would be troubled from the start. Her drug addiction would escalate and Jennings would express his own regret at marrying her.

"I don't know why I married her," Jennings said. "All she does is pop pills all day."

After less than three years of marriage, Velma decided to part ways with Jennings. She didn't file for divorce, however, she decided to poison him with arsenic. She would later claim that she only meant to "make him sick."

Jennings Barfield was already ill and doctors had no suspicion that Velma was behind the death. Arsenic was a slow burn poison that could kill without detection. The autopsy called for no arsenic test and Velma had gotten away with murder once again.

But Seven months later, Velma would overdose on her prescription meds and become hospitalized. Her family recognized the pattern but could not wean Velma off of the drinks. She would remain hospitalized for three weeks.

Her personality seemed to change after the hospital release. She returned to work at Belk department store but kept being combative and argumentative with customers. Her boss knew of her circumstances and tried to coax her to do better. He took her away from the public contact and into the back stock room where he had her put pricing on the clothing items.

Her boss soon realized that Velma's addiction had gotten out of control. Velma would not be able to function in the back room, leaving tasks uncompleted as she would have her prescription medications delivered to the store.

"It is a hopeless situation," the store manager told Velma's son Ronnie before he fired his mother.

BROKE AND DESTITUTE

With no income, Velma would lose the family home as she no longer paid the mortgage. She would be forced to move back in with her parents and face the two people she blamed everything for.

Her father had grown ill, however, and would die from lung cancer shortly after Velma moved back into the home. She would feel bad about her father's death and admit that she had a love/hate relationship with him.

"I had learned to love him as much as I had hated him," Velma said. "He was so good to my kids. I think he tried to do with my kids like he wished he had done to us. He could not stand to see me correct them. If I would pick them up and spank them, he would ask me, 'Isn't that enough?'"

But after her father's death Velma self-medicated once again. She overdosed and was hospitalized for two weeks. Her family didn't judge, they instead thought she was "cursed."

"Velma needed psychiatric help," Orange said. "So she began medicating herself with deleterious results. She would "doctor shop" for different physicians who would be manipulated into giving her the drugs she wanted. Her addiction eventually grows until she becomes desperate for money in order to fuel the drug habit."

A MURDERER AND A THIEF

Velma began stealing from those closest to her, starting with her mother. Her mother confronted Velma about a missing check and Velma went ballistic.

"She had violent mood swings," Orange said. "The medication had completely changed her personality as she needed the drugs above all else. The people around her were not familiar with how to handle a person who had this kind of mental illness. So this made for a very dangerous cocktail for her and anyone close to her."

Hitting a new low, Velma took out a $1,000 loan under her mother Lillie's name. She put up the family home as collateral and forged her mother's signature on the documents. Velma then blew through the money and a month later took out another loan, once again using her mother's house as collateral. The following month, she emptied the checking account on her now deceased husband, Jennings. Two months later, the loan company began sending Velma overdue notices as she had not been paying off the loan.

"In Velma's mind," Orange said. "She had no other choice but to kill off her own mother."

Velma went to the local pharmacy and looked for bottles that had the warning of "fatal if ingested." She put the poison into a drink for her mother and watched as she drank the fatal elixir.

Her mother then began vomiting and lost control of her bowels. Within a few hours, her mother could not so much as walk and an ambulance was called.

Velma came to visit her in the hospital to finish the job. Armed with a Thermos, she made a special concoction of chicken soup and arsenic.

"Drink it slow," Velma said as she tenderly lifted the cups to the lips of her ailing mother. "Slow."

Her mother would eventually die of "natural causes" as no one suspected Velma of committing murder. Instead, she received sympathy.

"So sorry for your loss," hospital staff said.

"The thing with arsenic is that it shuts down the whole system," Orange said. "So hospital staff just chalked up her mother's weakness to old age. Checking for arsenic poisoning would be the furthest thing from their mind."

Velma showed the necessary emotion and received sympathy from friends and family. She then moved in with her daughter Kim and son-in-law Dennis who lived in a trailer park. She could not evade the authorities for long though as the authorities caught wind of Velma's check forgeries.

Velma reacted as she always did. She would run away and medicate herself.

"Her drug addiction kept pushing her into a corner and she saw no way out," Orange said. "So, this time, she goes to her son Ronnie's house and overdoses again, trying to kill herself. She falls and breaks her collar bone which laid her out in the hospital another three weeks."

But the police find her situation unsympathetic.

"We're sorry, Velma," the deputy informed her at her hospital bed. "But once you have been cleared for release, we will arrest you."

Velma would not have that. She tried to overdose again but this go around the hospital staff pumped out her stomach.

She was sent to court the next day and sentenced to six months in jail for the forgery. She is released after four months for good behavior.

NO REHAB HERE

Her addiction still unchecked, Velma returned to live with Kim and her son-in-law. She rummaged through the belongings of her son-in-law and stole a check, forging his name so she can get more prescription meds. Her daughter Kim now has caught wind of her mother's addiction, pleading with her doctors to stop prescribing her.

"In some ways," Orange said. "The doctors were just as guilty as she was. But back in the day, there was no way to cross-reference this stuff like we do now. Once she had her fill with one doctor she would go to the next and the next."

Velma's addiction prevented her from taking a forty-hour a week job. So she looked for alternative forms of income.

She would find a job taking care of the elderly.

Montgomery and Dolly Edwards would be her first clients.

"She found herself some easy targets," Orange said. "There didn't seem to be any legislative body in place that prevents sociopaths from caretaking the elderly. So Velma doesn't slip through any cracks, she just befriends the elderly couple and begins taking care of them."

Montgomery was blind and unable to walk. He was 93-years old and his 83-year old wife was too feeble to take care of him. They paid $75 a week for Velma to become their live-in caretaker.

All was good, at least in the beginning. But Dolly had a sharp tongue and would criticize Velma daily. Velma would keep a nice exterior unless confronted, saw Dolly has yet another wheel in her cycle of verbal abuse.

"It seemed to be a never-ending loop for her," Orange said. "Being forced to deal with verbally abusive people. Velma had long since snapped and Dollie simply had no idea who she was dealing with."

Velma began to plot out Montgomery and Dollie's demise until she meets their nephew, Stuart Taylor.

Stuart was already married but was blown away when he met the caretaker of his Aunt Dollie.

Velma would play it cool, stealing what she could from the couple in terms of petty cash and household items that had value. They outlived their usefulness to her within a year as Montgomery died of "natural causes". One month later, Dolly also passed away.

And again, no one suspected the sweet and soft-spoken Velma to have had anything to do with their deaths.

MOVING ON

Velma saw being a caretaker as a perfect front for her. She could steal as much money as she could and when the old folks detected something amiss she would simply poison them. After killing the Edwards' couple, she set the word out at church that she as available to be a caregiver. The pastor would refer her to Margie Lee Pittman who was seeking for a caregiver for her elderly parents, John Henry and Record Lee.

"She comes here twice a week," the pastor reassured Pittman. "She's a nice, kindly woman. You can't go wrong."

Pittman's father, John Henry Lee, was eighty years old when he discovered that his new caregiver had forged a $50 check on his account. He then fell violently ill, suffering through a spastic spell of vomiting, diarrhea, and convulsions. The doctors would chalk up his quick death to gastroenteritis but in fact, he had been poisoned with arsenic.

Velma played the caregiver role until his end. She attended his funeral and cried with the family, sending an ornate wreath (with money stolen from the dead man) to the proceedings.

For whatever reason, Velma spared Lee's wife and moved back to Lumberton, North Carolina to live in a trailer park. She began working as an aide in a nursing home and received word from Stuart that he was now a widow. The two began dating and she moved part of her belongings into his home.

"Stuart is a nice guy," Orange said. "He has no idea what kind of woman Velma is. She is so manipulative and cunning that the younger man is putty in her hands. So the relationship starts great as she reels him in with kindness and charm."

The couple are happy cohabitating until Stuart Stuart finds a letter addressed to Velma from the state penitentiary.

Curious, he began reading the correspondence and realized that is from a former cellmate of Velma.

Stuart became enraged. He threatened to "expose" Velma to all of his family and friends. Somehow, someway, however, she was able to calm him down.

He then found out that she had forged over $200 in checks on his account. The two argued but stayed together for the next two months.

"Velma had the Christian facade down pat," Orange said. "She asked Stuart to forgive her and the next thing you know they are going to a Rex Humbard revival. But before they went, she poured arsenic poison in both his beer and tea. She made sure he drank every drop."

Returning home from the revival, Stuart started to vomit on the drive home, the poison kicking in.

Velma had to keep the con going. She had to appear like a concerned girlfriend so she called up Stuart's daughter, Alice, later that night and told her that Stuart had came down with the flu.

Stuart's daughter expressed concern but Velma kept her at bay.

"Don't you worry now, honey. I'll take care of everything."

Stuart died the next day.

Velma would speak at Stuart's funeral and tearfully asked for his wedding band. His family graciously allowed her to have it and gave her $400 to help her cope with the grief.

But Alice knew her father was a picture of health. She vociferously argued for more tests beyond the standard autopsy and sure enough, arsenic had been found in Stuart's tissues.

On March 10th, 1978, the sheriffs arrived at Velma's home to bring her in for questioning. She was interrogated for over three hours, holding her ground. But she knows the evidence will trump her denials and tries to commit suicide after being released. This go around, however, her son Ronnie stopped her.

The sheriffs come to visit Velma again and she has one more surprise up her sleeve.

But Velma has one more surprise up her sleeve.

She would confess. Not only for the murder of Stuart but of six others.

"I set my first husband on fire," Velma confessed without an attorney present. "And I killed the rest of them."

"It was almost as if she wanted to be free of the guilt she had been carrying," Orange said. "Her confession seemed to take a burden off her back."

"The last ten years were like that," Velma said. "A drug nightmare. It was a case of not knowing where you are or what you've done."

The bodies of her victims were later exhumed and all tested positive for arsenic.

FACING THE GRIM REAPER

Velma's case would be prosecuted by Joe Freeman Britt, who was listed in the Guinness Book of World Records as the country's "deadliest prosecutor."

Velma would plead not guilty by reason of insanity but the court denied her plea.

"I needed to keep them sick until I could pay back the money I had stolen from them," Velma said. "I wanted to earn their thanks by nursing them back to health. I needed the money. I was addicted to pain killers. Anti-depressants. Amphetamines."

On November 23rd, 1978, Velma's trial would begin in Elizabethtown, North Carolina where she would be charged with the first-degree murder of her boyfriend, Stuart Taylor. The trial lasted seven days and the jury reached a verdict of guilty, placing her on death row at the age of 47. She was scheduled to be executed on February 3rd, 1979 but received a stay.

Velma would be sentenced to death and the verdict was appealed all the way to the U.S. Supreme court. Her attorney maintained that the jury had never been presented with the full extent of Velma's "addiction and background." Velma remained tight-lipped about that to everyone but her pastor. Her attorney felt thought her horrific background could have been used as part of her defense and the jury would have found her to be more of a sympathetic case.

CHANGING SPOTS?

"She's not the same person who went to prison in 1978," Kim Burke Norton, Velma's daughter said.

While in jail, Velma became a model prisoner.

"The first week I was here was the worst week," Velma recalled. "Everything about it."

Velma no longer had access to her drugs in prison and she began to dry out. With daily visits from two different pastors, Velma began to discuss her anger and repressed issues that fueled her addiction and murders.

Velma would claim that as she was awaiting trial in 1978 she came to a "meeting with Christ" that caused her to "change inwardly."

Velma heard a broadcast by radio evangelist JK Kinkle. "Jesus loves you, prisoners, too," Kinkle said. "He died for you too. No matter what you've done, the Lord will forgive you."

After Velma heard this sermon, she dropped to her knees and cried out to God.

She would then become the "go to" counselor for young inmates in the prison.

The inmates would nickname Velma as "Mama Margie" because of her wisdom and she would in turn think of them as her "adopted children."

The prison guards and counselors would take the most incorrigible prisoners and place them in a cell next to Velma. Velma would invariably counsel the young prisoner and advise them on the correct path.

"They'd come in ready to kill themselves," Sister Mary Teresa Floyd said. "And here she was with a death sentence, mothering and helping them."

"Living in prison is a struggle," Velma said. "Even at its best. And I know that without Him and His strength that has sustained me, I couldn't have made it even this far."

Her stay on death row soon became a part of the news brief. During this time, a phalanx of evangelists would take her cause to the mainstream. The Reverend Hugh Hoyle would become Velma's personal minister as she received stays of execution in September, October and December of 1981. She would also have a letter correspondence with Ruth Graham, Billy Graham's wife as well as meeting their daughter Ann.

While Velma impressed the Christian do-gooders, the family members of the victims were not taken in by her "conversion."

"She's got religion now, they say," Margie Lee Pittman said. "Well, she had religion before. So we all thought."

A few more stays were granted until 1984 when the U.S. Supreme Court justice Warren Burger granted her a stay until August of that year. At this point, however, her execution seemed inevitable. In an ironic move, Velma would choose poison rather than the gas chamber and enjoyed the final visits from her children and grandchildren.

During the final week before her execution, the Reverend Hoyle, and his wife came to the prison with a battery-powered portable keyboard. His wife played the little organ then the Reverend sang "He Hideth My Soul" and "He is So precious to Me" in the cramped visitor booth.

Velma sang along, whistling in the graveyard before the reaper came for her.

She then wrote letters to each of the victim's family asking them for forgiveness. Reverend Hoyle would deliver the letters to the families, all of whom would refuse them.

MEET THE HANGMAN

As her execution date neared, Velma was placed in a solitary cell that stood directly across from the death chamber.

"It's total isolation," Velma said. "From everyone I had been with for six years."

North Carolina Governor James B.Hunt would reject her final plea for clemency.

On the day of her execution, the jail house would turn into a media frenzy. Death penalty advocates gathered outside the prison and chanted "Hip, hip, hurrah...K-I-L-L" while some sloganeered with "burn, bitch, burn". The protesters held up a few placards that quote Romans ch.13 which ironically was a verse that Velma would repeat to guards during her prison stay.

"For rulers are not a terror to good works, but to the evil...(The ruler) beareth no the sword in vain, for he is the minister of God, a revenger to execute wrath upon him that doeth evil."

The execution was scheduled to take place at 2:00 a.m but the protesters remained outside, their chants reduced to a simple "Kill her! Kill her!"

On November 2nd, 1984, Velma would be executed by lethal injection. The prison official came out and addressed the press, giving out copies of Barfield's statement of apology. The reporters then eagerly anticipated what Velma requested for her last meal. Initially, Velma just wanted the normally scheduled prison food; chicken livers, collard greens and a sheet cake with peanut butter icing. The last meal was delivered but Velma immediately lost her appetite. Instead, she opted for Cheese Doodles and a glass of Coca-Cola.

"Her attorney believed that Velma could have done some good in life," Orange said. "He stated that she could have become a teacher, counselor or a pastor. But her father set her on a path of self-destruction that she couldn't escape from. By the time she the left that road to ruin, she was too far gone in terms of her murderous acts. Justice had to be served in the end. In the end, the law doesn't care how genuine you are in your pleas for forgiveness. It only cares about the rule of law."

"I'm sorry for the hurt that I've caused," Velma said before her execution. "So many people, today if it were possible, I wish I could take every bit of hurt on myself."

quarters reporting the fire in the vacant lot. The caller investigated further, however, and saw Oscar's arm sticking out through the fire. He called 911 again with a sense of urgency, telling them of the body.

CHAPTER SIX

When police on scene identified Oscar Velazquez' partially burned body, their initial knee-jerk reaction was that this was the work of a local street gang, a drug deal gone awry. But when they found the nail polish remover bottle, however, they quickly realized that this was the work of amateurs. A jealous girlfriend maybe.

Meanwhile, the DeFrancisco sisters cruised around town over the following days, trying to pawn off the Camaro.

"This is where the sisters make the guys in 'Dumb and Dumber' look like geniuses," Clark said. "They had only pre-planned the front end of the murder. Like most impulsive killers, they had no idea what to do after. Their greed took over and they decide to sell the Camaro. They have no papers for it, duh, and really can only sell a stolen vehicle to a thug. They find no takers as even the dumbest street gang member isn't going to buy a hot car from two teenaged girls. So they cruise around town and Oscar's brother spots them in the car."

The girls, failing in their sales efforts, would later abandon he vehicle behind a storefront and set it on fire.

**

The day after Oscar's killing, a mutual friend named Jessica Benitez stopped by the house. Jessica went downstairs and watched Margaret mop up a stain of blood near the basement steps.

"The hell is that?" she asked.

Margaret said nothing as she poured bleach over the blood, scrubbing hard.

"Dude bled all over the floor," Regina said. "But only after Margaret kicked him in the head. We called him over, told this idiot we'd have a threesome with him. Then we robbed his ass."

"But the blood stain on the floor-" Jessica asked, watching Margaret clean up.

"We killed a guy," Margaret said without remorse.

"He was going to kill us!" Regina said. "Margaret shot him in the back of the head. We searched his body and found a gun in his waistband. Then we wrapped him up in plastic and put him in his car."

"Holy shit, girl," Jessica.

"We're about to go on the run," Margaret announced.

"Aren't you scared?" Jessica asked, looking back down at the blood stain in the basement.

"I ain't scared of nothing," Margaret said. "You should have seen his head when I shot him. His brain oozed out like cheese."

Margaret made a rolling motion with her hands.

Jessica then accompanied Margaret to the store she purchased a bottle of blonde hair dye for her "disguise."

"We see here how the whole street gang culture has influenced the behavior of these girls," Clark said. "At any point in time, Veronica or Jessica could have went straight to the police. But they get caught up in the drama of the moment. The so-called 'loyalty' to their friend who, quite frankly, would shoot them up in a heartbeat if they knew that they were going to be a snitch."

Going off the tip from Oscar's brother, the police show up to question both Regina and Margaret. The duo denied ever seeing Oscar.

They then go to interview Veronica Garcia.

They found the jittery fifteen year old to be a different story, however. The teen quickly crumbled under the pressure of questioning and told the police the entire story.

Feeling the heat, the DeFrancisco sisters go on the run...

CHAPTER SEVEN

For all of their stupidity in committing the murder, the DeFrancisco sisters deftly avoided capture for almost two years.

They decided to split up. Margaret would go to live with their maternal aunt in Roscoe, Illinois, an hour and a half drive away from where they lived. Roscoe was a small town with less then 10,000 people, a far cry from the drug infested streets of Chicago. Margaret's worst dreams were now realized. She was now a nerd who had to stay inside all day long, living in a boring cul-de-sac with no street gang action. Neighbors would remark that they would never see her and if hey did she would quickly go back inside.

Living underground without detection, it took a broadcast of the television show AMERICA'S MOST WANTED to generate an anonymous tip which led to Margaret's whereabouts. Police staked out her aunt's apartment and entered, finding Margaret in her bedroom with a blank look on her face.

"My feelings were hurt bad because she (my wife) did something behind my back," Margaret's uncle by marriage said later. "I knew (police) were going to find her anyway."

Seven months later, Regina was captured in Dallas living with her Latin King boyfriend, Johnny Rivera.

Initially, she did not even know where the gang banger lived. She just knew the town, Laredo, and she journeyed there by bus. Regina would eventually find him, locating one of his relatives. She would live under an alias and claimed that she worked as a maid.

Police knew better. Regina made money by selling drugs under the Latin King banner.

Unlike Margaret, Regina had evaded the scrutiny of the America's Most Wanted viewers.

Her capture came about because she could not stop hanging out with the wrong crowd.

Two sheriffs were had mistakenly arrived at her boyfriend's apartment, wanting to serve a warrant to someone else.

Rivera allowed the deputies to enter his apartment but he had left a marijuana flake on his table. Police searched the apartment further and found several packages of crack cocaine ready to be sold.

The deputies arrested Rivera. They searched inside the apartment and interviewed Regina, who was groggy from a cocaine high. She showed them her false Texas identification and they let her go.

But the deputies smelled something fishy on her aside from marijuana. They had the apartment manager set up a meeting with her. She arrived at the complex in an SUV with another man. The police approached and the SUV sped away.

The high-speed chase down residential Dallas streets reached upwards of 90 mph. The SUV then slammed into a center median, the front tires blowing out.

Regina got out of the car and tried to sprint away. A deputy tackled her and they fell to the ground, her cell phone skidding across the gravel road. Sifting through her pockets, the officer found over $1,500 cash.

She was taken to Dallas County Jail where they discovered her true identity.

"We pulled her out of jail," said a Deputy Dodson. "I asked to see one of her tattoos, and she showed me...I called her by name, but she never said a word to me. She knew it was over."

She was then extradited to Illinois to stand trial for the murder of Oscar Velazquez.

CHAPTER EIGHT

The trial of the two women began in July of 2004 and both sisters pleaded not guilty by reason of self-defense.

But their friend, Veronica Garcia, had cut a deal with prosecutors in return for a lesser sentence. She would provide the testimony that would damn the two sisters to prison.

Garcia said that she didn't know what the sisters had planned. She had simply provided the gun to the DeFrancisco's which she thought would be used for a robbery only.

"I didn't see her shoot Oscar," Veronica said.

The prosecution brought forth additional witnesses in Jessica Benitez, Luciana Macias, and Maria Constantino, the neighbor.

"Both of them told me that they killed Oscar," Jessica said. "Margaret kicked him in the head so he could die faster."

"I saw them load the body into the back of the Camaro," Constantino said. "Regina told me that she planned out the killing."

Margaret, however, maintained their innocence. She said that Oscar came to the apartment angry because the sisters had tricked him out of one-thousand dollars.

"I shot him to protect Regina," Margaret said.

"Then why didn't you tell the reporting officer what happened?" the prosecution attorney asked.

"We would've got in trouble," Margaret said. "If I told the truth, I would've been there longer."

Regina DeFrancisco would also take the stand and claim self-defense as well.

"I came out of my bedroom," Regina said. "And he was there, cursing and screaming. He pulled a gun on me. I thought I was going to die. I curled up on the floor, in a fetal position. I begged for my life. Then I heard a gunshot and saw Margaret standing over Oscar, holding a gun."

"Whose idea was it to dispose of the body?"

"Veronica knew of this vacant lot," Regina said. "It was her idea."

The jury would deliberate for over six and a half hours. Regina would be found guilty of murder. Margaret's jury, however, was unable to convict her. There was and 11 to 1 deadlock with one juror believing that she should be acquitted. The juror did not believe that someone so young could commit murder.

Margaret was then released from custody and told to await retrial. She had a baby during this time, a girl, and would find work as a nursing assistant while she awaited another trial.

Four months later, Margaret would be given another day in court. Veronica Garcia would once again be the star witness for the prosecution, detailing the exact same testimony as before.

There would be no deadlock in this second go around as Margaret would be convicted of first-degree murder.

Regina would be sentenced to 35 years in prison while Margaret would be sentenced to 46 years. Both women are now jailed at the Dwight Correctional Center. They have each filed appeals which have been denied.

"The girls cared nothing about Oscar Velazquez," Clark said. "In the end, they remained true to their own narcissistic nature. They only cared about what was happening to the next. They cared about nothing about the now fatherless children Oscar Velazquez would leave behind nor about the fact that the took his life."

Veronica Garcia was jailed for five years. She served her full sentence and has since been released.

"This is a cautionary tale if there ever was one," Clark said. "The sisters had it all. They had access to one of the finest schools in their state. Yet they chose to throw it all away for short money and the cheap thrill of the 'thug life.' In the end, they got to see what the 'thug life' was really all about. Mindless violence where everyone is out for themselves, especially when there is a plea bargain to be made. They could have had it all had they stayed on the straight and narrow. Now they have nothing."